AI, AR, AND VR IN THEATRE AND PERFORMANCE

AI, AR, and VR in Theatre and Performance investigates the cutting-edge application of evolving digital technologies within the creative industries, with a focus on theatre and the dramatic arts.

Grounded in a practice-based approach, this book explores the experiences of creatives, producers, and IT-specialist content creators employing artificial intelligence (AI), augmented reality (AR), and virtual reality (VR) technologies. A series of international case studies are presented, demonstrating current techno-infused practices, as well as potential futures for these technologies within the broadest of creative contexts. Framed by a rigorous ethnodramatic methodological approach, the book examines the practical applications of contemporary digital technologies in theatre and other live performance settings and provides a scaffolding framework for readers to adopt in their own practice. It also proposes groundbreaking ideas for the classification of how AI may be used in current and future artistic practices, the 'three Cs of AI,' and introduces the concept of Communal Augmented Reality – Live (CARL) as the most likely form to advance the incorporation of emerging technologies onto the live stage. The works of Belgium's VR immersive experiences company CREW, Singapore-based film and visual artist Ho Tzu Nyen, and the Tamil language theatre company AGAM Theatre Lab are detailed alongside the world-first application of AR holographic technology in Australia, before unpacking the pioneering advancements in algorithmic and AI theatre of America's Annie Dorsen.

With a practice-based, artist-led perspective and contributions from technologists, this book offers a comprehensive and accessible resource that will appeal to a diverse audience of artists, academics, students, practitioners, creative engineers/content creators, animators, and theorists with an interest in the relationship between digital technologies and live performance.

Shane Pike, PhD, is a senior lecturer in the School of Creative Arts at the Queensland University of Technology. An award-winning producer, writer, and director of theatre, his most recent works fuse traditional practices with emerging technologies. He is also a Chief Investigator on the Australian Research Council-funded project Advancing Digital Innovation in the Australian Live Performance Sector, partnering with Australia's leading performing arts institutions to develop sustainable digital strategies for the future of live arts.

AI, AR, AND VR IN THEATRE AND PERFORMANCE

Technology in the Present and Future of Live Creative Arts

Shane Pike

NEW YORK AND LONDON

Designed cover image: Jeanda St James rehearsing behind the Hologauze in *Alex: A Play with Holograms.* Photo by Zachary Boulton.

First published 2026
by Routledge
605 Third Avenue, New York, NY 10158

and by Routledge
4 Park Square, Milton Park, Abingdon, Oxon, OX14 4RN

Routledge is an imprint of the Taylor & Francis Group, an informa business

ISBN: 978-1-032-86225-5 (hbk)
ISBN: 978-1-032-86224-8 (pbk)
ISBN: 978-1-003-52190-7 (ebk)

DOI: 10.4324/9781003521907

Typeset in Galliard
by SPi Technologies India Pvt Ltd (Straive)

CONTENTS

ACKNOWLEDGEMENTS

Thank you to Yoko Tanaka, the Queensland University of Technology, particularly the Faculty of Creative Industries, Education and Social Justice, and the School of Creative Arts, their Executive Dean and Head of School, and the Design Lab and its Centre Director, Prof. Evonne Miller, for supporting this research and the project that makes up its opening case study. Thank you also to the Batchelor family, Brisbane City Council and Arts Queensland for providing critical funding to novel experiments in technology and live performance that made this work possible. Eric Joris; The Doodle People's Lynnette Ee, Timothi Lim, Saskia Bünte and Ivan Liew; Subramanian Ganesh and Nallu Dhinakharan from AGAM Theatre; and Ho Tzu Nyen must also be acknowledged, for the time and consideration given to participating in this research so openly and generously, and for their unending dedication and magnificent contributions to the arts and its ongoing evolution. I would also like to thank Jeffrey Tan, Kyueun Kim, and Dane Antala, for providing critical guidance and insight into tech-infused creative practices across the region, sharing their time, expertise, and networks to welcome me so warmly to Singapore – and for their own magnificent contributions to the arts, technology, and arts research on a global scale. Lastly, to the core creative team behind *Alex: A play with holograms* – Elizabeth Gibbs, Kathryn Kelly, Tessa Rixon, Paul Van Opdenbosch, Freddy Komp, Zachary Boulton, Jeanda St James, Jag Popham, Travis Macfarlane, Harley Coustley and his team, Maxi Mossman, and Cameron Grimmett – a very big thank you.

1

INTRODUCTION

Backstory, context, and the cases studied

Developments in technology continue unabated. What this means for art, artists, and human creativity is an ongoing discussion, particularly when considering advancements in areas such as artificial intelligence, and whether such technology will ultimately be found to *enhance* or altogether *replace* the role and work of the artist. For live, performing arts, there are specific considerations around the evolution of emerging technologies and how this is impacting the development, realisation, and consumption of the artform by artists and audiences alike. While some may see this as a continuation of established dialogue around the impact of digital, programmable and recordable practices on live arts events, the advent of technology's ability not just to *record* and *replay* but also potentially *create* provides new opportunities for discussion and investigation. In any case, considerations around technology and live creative expressions, further disrupted during the COVID-19 pandemic and its accompanying quarantining of live arts to the online world, are not entirely settled. It is pertinent to take stock of the current landscape and identify whether and/or how technology is impacting theatre and live performance in an ongoing capacity.

Artificial Intelligence (AI), Augmented Reality (AR), and Virtual Reality (VR) are chosen as the focus for this book, as they represent the most potential for change in how theatre and live performance may be presented and experienced by artists and audiences in the future. As demonstrated in the historiography chapter, VR is the most established of the three technologies in its application in a live performance context and, therefore, provides a solid test-case for how artists might adopt and adapt to emerging technologies in their practices. Ultimately, it is shown that VR technology lends itself

DOI: 10.4324/9781003521907-1

most usefully to immersive experiences, while AI and AR show potential to enhance or alter a more traditional theatre/live performance experience. While AR does also demonstrate a practicality in creating immersive environments, its potential to augment and evolve the visual world-making effects of a traditional theatre work presents the greatest opportunity. This is rendered most evident in the possibility for AR to create "Communal Augmented Reality – Live" experiences, preserving the liveness of the form while enabling fantastic visual and other effects to populate the physical, as opposed to virtual, onstage world.

In the case of AI, this technology presents opportunities to both generate creative content and also enhance and streamline the creative process for artists and makers. It is shown that AI is already being used to create theatre – generating scripts, enhancing voices in musical theatre, producing images for marketing content – but has latent potential to also improve the workflow of existing practices. If AI can be paired with AR to improve virtual production systems, for example, the possibilities to incorporate animated and other digital enhancements into the live performance outcome are seemingly endless. This facilitates the advent of the next wave of innovation in onstage design and scenographic enhancement. So, while large language models and natural language programmes such as ChatGPT, Microsoft CoPilot, DeepSeek and Meta's llama – or whatever has been released in the last five minutes since this has been read – are relevant and currently occupy a large part of the general AI discourse among the broader community, their influence on theatre and live performance is only one element for consideration.

It is time to take stock of how evolutions in AI, AR, VR, and the technologies they represent are impacting the artform and being adopted by makers to explore the opportunities, challenges and influences they are having on live arts practices. This includes considering issues around accessibility and bias that are found to be inherent in some of the technologies and their enabling devices. There is also a consistent reference to infrastructural investment and institutional resources, identified by most contributing case studies, that must be addressed to enable theatre and live performance to more easily pursue a technologically enhanced future and provide the highest quality outcomes for makers and their audiences. Evaluating the technologies through a practice-led methodological approach, ensures art and art makers remain at the centre of the discussion, placing the outcomes of their experiences and experiments with technology as influential to any predictions about how a future might look in a world where computer-based programmes and systems are able to replicate and even generate examples of the once-considered human-only expression of creativity.

For the subject of one case study chapter, CREW founder, Eric Joris, the point in time we find ourselves is analogous to the early days of cinema, where filmmakers experimented with narrative forms and technological processes before arriving at the now-established conventions, techniques and creative and practical lexicon that defines the form and enables it to function within its own accepted ecology. In the same way that the language of filmmaking developed over time – moving from static camera shots to complex, dynamic cinematography – it is arguable that VR/AR/AI theatre needs time to experiment and refine its own techniques. We are at the point of experimentation not only to discover *how* to make the technology work, but to understand *why* it works and how audiences respond to it. This process is crucial to developing theatre and live performance practices sustainably alongside technology, allowing for the accepted integration of digital and live elements. This book is a contribution to this broader discussion, uniquely drawing upon real-world examples from practicing artists to identify how they are managing technological developments within their field.

This document and the studies it includes do not wish to date nor time-capsule current practices, but to comprehend how the field has and is evolving, extrapolating from existing practices, as a moment in time, that can be used to assist in the ongoing framing, categorising and developing of both theory and practice into the future. This work contributes to the growing research area of technology and live performance. With current examples chosen from a global field of academic and practitioner contributions, it is hoped it will serve to capture a key moment in time for developments in the world's cultural and creative industries. The lessons gained and understandings made through the case studies of this collection are applicable for ongoing experimentations and may serve as a foundation for the unending evolution of creative expressions embedding elements of the technological. By analysing the use of technology in these real-world situations, lessons are provided for other artists and makers to incorporate technology into their own processes, and possible future opportunities are identified for further experimentation with emerging technologies in live performance.

Intersecting notions of digital theatre, intermedial performance, theatre and globalisation through technology, live versus digital arts and the place of creative practice in a digital and AI revolution, it is hoped this contribution will complement other offerings in the field. Employing a practice-led, ethnodramatic methodological approach to generate a detailed investigation that premises creative practices and the place of the artist alongside the technologist, and not in competition, this monograph intends to serve makers, thinkers, designers, engineers, artists, students, academics and practitioners alike. The conflating of theatre, performance, arts, artists, creative arts and live arts and the sometimes interchangeable use of these terms may irk some definitional and classificational purists, however, it should also serve to highlight the inter- and cross-disciplinary realities of working with art and technology. This also aligns with the reality of many of those working in the sector, including artists interviewed as part of this research, who declare that the definition of form is far less interesting to them than the exploration of forms in the plural that is enabled by the technology.

The impetus behind this book was a body of practice-led research focusing on the use of emerging technologies in live theatre. However, as the research unfolded, the notions of theatre and liveness regularly demonstrated broader considerations across artforms, particularly where the subsuming of technology into creative practices was evidenced. So, while there is a focus on theatre and theatre makers, the fundamental ideas and applications underpinning this investigation are conceivably applicable across the spectrum of creative arts experiences, particularly those produced with an aspect of liveness. In a similarly expansive approach, the opening historiography applies a broad definition of technology, drawing on examples across the history of live theatre and performance, from the amphitheatres of Ancient Greece to the online and digital stages of today. Case study examples include diverse instances of mainstream commercial theatre, site-specific immersive art experiences, online dance productions and works that blur the boundaries between visual art installation and theatrical encounter.

Evidencing elements of theatre, film, dance, visual arts, digital arts, and even creative writing – through the themes of AI and its application in generating written narratives – the examples and discussions in the following chapters demonstrate the interdisciplinarity inherent in many examples of the fusion between technology and creativity. The theatre, then, is employed as the artistic through-line not only because, as the writer, I am a theatre maker but also, as the brief historiography of theatre and technology demonstrates in Chapter 1, theatre has a long history of capitalising on advances in technology (Tompkins, 2016) and adopting innovations from other artforms: visual arts in scenography and stage design, music not only in soundscape and effects but also the musical theatre form, poetry and story in its narratives, film and digital arts and design within the concept of intermedial theatre. A basis in theatre, then, seems as justifiable a position as any.

Following the succinct historical account of technology with theatre and live performance at the outset, the proceeding chapters each focus on examples demonstrating the use of AI, AR and/or VR technology in a real-world context. The first, *Alex: A play with holograms* is a commercial theatre production incorporating AR effects, presented at La Boite Theatre Company in Brisbane, Australia. This is a firsthand account, written as a reflection of the experience, producing what is believed to be a world-first in the way it applied holographic animations in its specific theatrical context, introducing the concept of Communal Augmented Reality – Live. This is followed by a discussion of the works of CREW, the world-renowned VR experiences company based in Brussels, Belgium. The chapter is predicated on an interview with CREW's founder, Eric Joris, and touches upon several of their productions to explore more deeply immersive theatre/experiences and the place of VR technology to create these environments. A framework for adopting technologies into practice, drawing from some of Joris's philosophies, experiences and lessons from a successful career fusing technology and live performance, is provided.

Then, a chapter stemming from interviews conducted with experimenters in art and technology, all based in Singapore. Saskia Bünte and Ivan Liew, producers from the mixed reality and interactive experiences company, The Doodle People, which created the virtual dance and theatre performance, *KINetic*, and the AR play, 拜拜年 *Bai Bai Nian* (*Happy New Year*). Subramanian Ganesh and Nallu Dhinakharan, respectively the Founder and Non-Executive Director of the company, AGAM Theatre Lab, who produced the world's first Tamil language AR play. And world-renowned visual and film artist, creative philosopher Ho Tzu Nyen, responsible for several award-winning, internationally touring AR and VR experiences. The ideas, notions, challenges and potential futures for the fusion of technology and performance that emerged from these interviews are discussed.

Elements such as passion, communication and shared interest, commercial imperatives, and critical cultural engagement are identified as key components to successful collaborations between technologists and artists. There is also discussion around live performance experiences and gaming, providing distinction and differentiation between each from the point of view of the technologists. It is in this chapter that the artist as an entrepreneur is most evident, and the connections between the technology industry and the arts are most distinguished. Highlighted, is the need for commercial and economic imperatives to be considered for continued experimentation with art and technology – as well as sustainability and the social, cultural, and environmental considerations technology raises and can address – if theatre and live performance are to be active participants in an evolving, tech-driven future. The value of arts to technology and other sectors is also highlighted, reinforcing the relationship as a quid-pro-quo and not simply a case of technology being able to enhance art. A significant element of this chapter is a focus on technology and agency, uncovering the more philosophical considerations around the use of emerging digital tools on the human condition and experience. Three further examples of an AR experience, a VR performance and a traditional exhibition attended in Singapore are also discussed to identify how each experience may provide a different encounter for audiences, based on the type of technology used.

Finally, AI and its application in live performance contexts is explored. The Three Cs of AI are discussed, providing a set of clear categories, in which all current and future uses of AI in theatre and live performance can be classified: AI as creative, AI as collaborator, and AI as concept. It is also proposed that these classifications can be transferred across non-performative artforms and non-creative sectors. Then, chiefly through the works of American maker, Annie Dorsen, the history of AI in theatre is investigated, including the ethical, moral and philosophical implications of the themes this artist explores. Early iterations experimenting with algorithmic theatre are briefly discussed, linked to more recent expressions of AI theatre, using large language models and other AI-powered computer programmes to generate and even present creative content in a live performance context.

A short conclusion is then offered, attempting to consolidate the most useful findings arising from the interviews and reflections, as well as positing potential futures for the place of AR, VR and AI within the live theatre and performance frame. This includes a section of the conclusion written by AI itself, as a light-hearted experiment with a large language model.

Technology, liveness, participant, audience, art, and theatre – Some definitions and frequently used terms

In the widest context of this book, the term 'technology' may encompass a broad spectrum of tools, systems and processes that influence, or have some kind of impact on, the production and delivery of a live, creative artwork. In the examples provided in the following chapters, that is usually a type of performance delivered to an audience by virtue of a performance space, or stage, which can be physical or virtual. The influence, or place, of the technology is not confined to the events, objects and bodies onstage, but may also affect the audience and their perception, or reception, of the artistic event. Indeed, in many cases, the utilisation of technology in a theatrical event, for example, is designed to enhance the impact of the story on an audience. This definition of technology also recognises recent computer-driven innovations not merely as a set of tools, but as an increasingly integral component of art-making that shapes the creative, performative and audience-interactive aspects of live performance events. As scholars like Steve Dixon (2007) argue, technology is both an enabler and a medium, redefining the boundaries of performance and challenging traditional notions of liveness, presence, and the human-technology interface.

Historically, then, technology in live performance has referred to mechanical, and later electrical, innovations such as stage machinery, lighting, visual, and sound systems that enable more dynamic and precise control of the performance environment. (Salter, 2010) However, with the advent of digital computer technologies, the term has expanded to include digital media, software, and interactive systems that facilitate new forms of storytelling and enable new possibilities for audience interaction. While it is acknowledged that the term technology is potentially broad and has meant different things to the live performance landscape throughout its history, as demonstrated in the concise historiography of theatre presented at the outset of this publication, a narrower understanding is applied as the discussion progresses and the case studies are extrapolated.

Outside the broad understanding applied in the historiographic account, then, the word 'technology' is largely understood as a reference to more recent digital and computer-driven innovations that form the substantive title of this book: Artificial Intelligence (AI), Augmented Reality (AR) and Virtual Reality (VR). Technology can refer to these things as overall concepts, elements of their practical application, as well as the equipment, hardware and software, required to use them. Further, technology is no longer exclusively a tool to manipulate the physical performance environment but has evolved to also be an instrument of creativity itself. Notably, in the case of AI, technology has the potential not only as a device, but as a generator – or creator – of art borne from the simplest of human prompts. Conceivably, this is the advent of a reality where even human intervention in the form of an inciting prompt may not be required, posing an unknown variety of possible futures concerning how, where and when our post-now selves may generate, experience and consume live arts with technology.

The concept of 'liveness' should also be mentioned as a key component of the discussion that follows. Confirmed by the case studies, the element of liveness provides the foundations of the dramatic/theatrical form and differentiates it from other examples of entertainment and creative expression, such as film. Liveness is not an element of traditional theatre that is simply being held on to from the past, but a defining attribute that can be leveraged to transform digital/digitised entertainment more generally. Ultimately, it is found that liveness is key to the ongoing adoption of emerging technology into the artform, with the potential for AR, for example, to enhance the theatrical event notably through its possibilities for liveness, in what is identified as Communal Augmented Reality – Live. Philosophies concerning 'live' and art and performance and how digital technologies and media have impacted the concept are keenly explored by far more authoritative thinkers than I (Auslander, 2012, 2022; Chapple & Kattenbelt, 2006; Dixon, 2007; Meyer-Dinkgräfe, 2015; Phelan, 1993). However, for the purposes of this account, live and liveness can be considered the requirement for the creative event to be performed in real time, with the audience and performers experiencing the work at the same time. This differentiates from an entirely filmic experience, where the performers record scenes, which are then produced and edited separately from their showing to an ultimately intended audience at a later date.

This is also different from a recorded live event, such as a theatrical performance or dance presentation that is videoed, digitised and then catalogued for audiences to view at another point in time. Though, the latter example may have initially been a live event when it was originally captured for digitisation. Acknowledging that components of AR and VR and other mediated live works, may also include pre-recorded performances and other elements, it can be understood that the substantive performance event takes place in real time to be experienced by the performer and audience synchronously. The audience and performers need not be located in the same physical space, though from a live theatre perspective, it is argued that co-location is ideal even though it is not a necessity.

The term 'artist' is also frequently used to describe a variety of creative roles. It can be understood to include theatre makers, directors, actors, and designers as well as musicians and choreographers while also maintaining its traditional associations with those otherwise known as visual artists. This list is not exhaustive, and context may provide the term descriptive of other roles within any particular creative example. There are also frequent references to 'traditional theatre,' which is understood as mainstream theatre practices that may use more established technologies – such as stage mechanics, lighting, sound, and to a certain extent, AV effects – but notably do not include elements of AI, AR, nor VR. References to the 'theatre,' 'theatrical,' 'dramatic,' 'works,' and 'creative events' are often generally indicating the performance of plays, though their genre and form may be a variety of classifications and can also, where context dictates, refer to multi- and interdisciplinary examples that may not be plays. The terms 'audience' and 'participant' are also found interchangeably, particularly throughout the discussion of immersive experiences.

Brief explanation of methodology

In practice, I am a playwright and theatre director. I often work in specific areas of the applied theatre form, namely Johnny Saldaña's (2011) version of ethnodrama and ethnotheatre (See also: Lewis et al., 2023; Pike, 2013, 2017a, 2017b, 2018, 2019; Pike et al., 2020). Ethnodrama can be understood as both the process and product of collecting ethnographic data to generate a playscript, while ethnotheatre is the production/performance of the ethnodramatic script. Data is collected for the script from a variety of means, which may include "selections from interview transcripts, field notes, journal entries, or other written artefacts" (Saldaña, 2003, p. 218). I have employed the same methodological approach to the development of this research monograph, interviewing participants, collecting notes from field trips to participant locations and conducting broader desktop research relevant to each chapter, sourcing data from academic, industry, creative, commercial and government-produced, written artefacts. The key difference being, rather than synthesising that data into an ethnodramatic playscript to be performed as an ethnotheatrical production, it has been interpreted as a research document to be published as a printed monograph. If Saldaña were to question the application of his framework in this way – to generate a book rather than a playscript – I humbly apologise.

This approach often requires multiple participant accounts and other contributions to be synthesised into a more singular voice, represented through common themes and experiences identified across the data that are subsequently expressed within a unified, dramatic narrative. In this spirit, the interviews conducted as part of the data-gathering process for the case studies are not recounted through direct quotations in a question-answer style format. They have been choreographed into a singular piece of prose that expresses the general themes and points made by each participant, including some direct quotes, interspersed with my own thoughts and mus- ings inspired by the conversations. This also results in each section adopting a slightly different voice/tone, influenced by each contributor, inevitably shaping the source interview along their own lines of thought and interest, encapsulating the specific creative and cultural ecology that supports their lived experiences. All participants were provided with copies of their rele- vant chapters prior to publication, and given the opportunity to confirm, check, correct and/or make any changes to their associated sections and how they have been represented.

Partly, the aims of this book are to identify and document how working performing artists are dealing with/adapting to new and emerging tech- nologies in their practice. Capturing this kind of lived experience lends itself well to an ethno-research form. My own background in ethnodrama, as a researcher and practitioner, is also relevant to the subject matter of this book. The interest is in the practical application of the technology and how that is evidenced in the work and has evolved through experience. Also notable about a Saldañaian approach, is the place of the researcher within the research. Removing them from the results is an impossible task, as the one who interprets the data is only able to understand it through their own perception and conception of the world. The researcher's experience, then, enables a deeper insight into the subject matter, particularly when they are a part of the community/experience that is under investigation. Included as a case study is one of my own works embedding augmented reality technol- ogy into the dramaturgical world-making. This direct experience with tech- nology in performance, enables a unique further investigation through the accompanying case studies, generating a level of understanding and shared experience between myself as author and other contributing artists as co-participants. This positions not only my self-reflective chapter, but also the book overall, to uncover unique insights about the use and usefulness of technology to live creative experiences.

A note on diversity and bias

As a person from a diverse background, in my work as a theatre writer, director, and researcher, it has always been an aim to also diversify the art that I make and study. With this in mind, it has been a further objective to include case studies from a global pool of practitioners, which has resulted in examples from Australia, Asia, Europe and North America. The Australian case study, *Alex: A Play with Holograms*, is also considered a Chinese-Australian work and was produced with principles of diversity in casting for the premiere production that is the subject of the study. The chapter based in Singapore, includes artists working across the region, from Singapore to South Korea and Japan, as well as an in-depth focus on a Tamil language theatre company. Another case study, CREW, while firmly in the Western sphere, is interestingly not an Anglo-Celtic/American company.

Ideally, it would be possible to include examples from all continents, particularly Africa and South America, which are notably absent. Perhaps future editions could be extended and resourced to include a truly holistic set of global examples. It is also notable that, in the case of AR at least, the historiography shows artists and technologists from Australia, Singapore and Canada are credited as the first adopters of the technology into live performance, with collaborations between US and European companies bringing the concept into the mainstream. Considering this, a focus on Australian, Singaporean, European and US case studies is defensible.

In a chapter titled "Dethroning Ourselves from the Centre," dramaturg Philipa Kelly (2020) declares that, like King Lear in the play of his name, it is time for the white, entitled world to de-centre itself from its dramaturgical throne. In the same publication, Annalisa Dias calls for a decolonising of theatre practice, warning that considerations of equity, diversity and inclusion are not enough "to save us from the violence of global white supremacy" (2020, p. 89). With this in mind, I also note the colonial and cultural bias inherent in some of the themes of the following chapters, particularly the focus on the development of technology and theatre from a predominantly Western perspective, for want of a better term.

The traceable roots of technological innovation in theatre as it is understood for the purposes of this book are demonstrably said to be grounded in ancient Greece and Rome. Not to mention, the terms technology and theatre and live performance themselves are grounded in colonial, Eurocentric understandings. This neglects the rich cultural and artistic traditions of African, Middle and Eastern spheres, but also most notably in my Australian context, the world's oldest continuous living culture: Australia's First Nations People. This book was predominantly written on the lands of the Turrbal, North of Meanjin (Brisbane). I was born on the lands of the Kanamaluka, on the island of Lutruwita (Tasmania), where traditions of storytelling and innovations in technology have existed for many tens of thousands of years.

We should also consider accessibility and the implicit bias in the technologies that form part of this discussion. As articulated at various points within the case studies, examples of AI through large language models and image-generating software are proven to perpetuate racial and cultural stereotypes, as well as lean towards gendered characterisation while favouring Western concepts and traditions of hegemonic masculinity. Virtual and AR equipment is also exclusive – motion capture suits and software are pre-programmed to identify the able-bodied male physique as a default. AR hardware, particularly wearable devices, is ineffective for those with low or no vision and proven to be difficult for the very young and the very old to wear without pain or discomfort. These issues of accessibility and bias appear frequently throughout the following chapters and should remain an important consideration in any application of new technologies in live performance.

Concluding the introduction

This book offers a unique insight into the use of AI, AR and VR technologies within theatre and other live arts experiences, from the point of view of the practitioners themselves. Through a series of globally significant case studies, how the technologies are used is detailed alongside some of the challenges that result from that utilisation, as well as offering predictions for future opportunities to embed technology within artforms. Attention is also given to the practical application, infrastructural requirements and applied use of technology, as well as – particularly where AI is concerned – the conceptual, social, cultural, philosophical and political considerations of adopting these technologies into the arts and society more generally.

Through ethnodramatic methods, the experiences and experimentations of artists and technologists with technology are documented, resulting in several key points for other makers to adapt into their own practices, consequently generating a framework for embedding these technologies into live performance. The reflective nature of the research also produces influential discussion around the possible futures for live performance, promoting an evolution of art that embraces the new and adopts technology's potential for its own benefit and advancement.

References

Auslander, P. (2012). Digital Liveness: A Historico-Philosophical Perspective. *PAJ: A Journal of Performance and Art, 34*(3), 3–11. https://www.jstor.org/stable/26206427

Auslander, P. (2022). *Liveness: Performance in a Mediatized Culture.* Taylor & Francis Group. https://ebookcentral.proquest.com/lib/qut/detail.action?docID=7127484

Chapple, F., & Kattenbelt, C. (2006). *Intermediality in Theatre and Performance.* Brill. https://ebookcentral.proquest.com/lib/qut/detail.action?docID=6914018

Dias, A. (2020). Decolonizing "equity, diversity, and inclusion" Strategies for resisting white supremacy. In P. Kelly (Ed.), *Diversity, Inclusion, and Representation in Contemporary Dramaturgy: Case Studies from the Field.* Taylor & Francis Group. https://ebookcentral.proquest.com/lib/qut/detail.action?docID=6144807

Dixon, S. (2007). *Digital Perfoermance: A History of New Media in Theater, Dance, Performance Art, and Installation.* MIT Press. https://ebookcentral.proquest.com/lib/qut/detail.action?docID=3338680

Kelly, P. (2020). Dethroning ourselves from the center. In P. Kelly (Ed.), *Diversity, Inclusion, and Representation in Contemporary Dramaturgy: Case Studies from the Field.* Taylor & Francis Group. https://ebookcentral.proquest.com/lib/qut/detail.action?docID=6144807

Lewis, C., Miller, E., & Pike, S. (2023). Writing research-based theatre on aged care: The ethnodrama, After Aleppo. *Culture and Organization,* ahead-of-print(ahead-of-print), 1–18. https://doi.org/10.1080/14759551.2023.2216829

Meyer-Dinkgräfe, D. (2015). Liveness: phelan, auslander, and after. *Journal of Dramatic Theory and Criticism, 29*(2), 69–79. https://doi.org/10.1353/dtc.2015.0011

Phelan, P. (1993). *Unmarked: The Politics of Performance.* Taylor & Francis Group. https://ebookcentral.proquest.com/lib/qut/detail.action?docID=179272

Pike, S. (2013). A role to play: Investigating concepts of masculinity in Australia through theatre. In Julie Lunn, Stephanie Bizjak, Sue Summers (Eds), *Chnging Facts, Changing Minds, Changing Worlds.* Black Swan Press.

Pike, S. (2017a). Articulating the Inarticulate: Performance and intervention in masculine gender (re)presentation. *Social Alternatives, 36*(2), 48–54. https://www.proquest.com/scholarly-journals/articulating-inarticulate-performance/docview/1953813687/se-2?accountid=13380

Pike, S. (2017b). *The boys of St Crispian.* Playlab. https://apt.org.au/product/the-boys-of-st-crispian-2/

Pike, S. (2018). *Nineteen.* Playlab. https://playlabtheatre.com.au/shop-publications/playlab-indie/nineteen-by-shane-pike/

Pike, S. (2019). "Make it so": Communal augmented reality and the future of theatre and performance. *Fusion Journal*(15), 108–118. https://doi.org/10.3316/informit.975162255148822

Pike, S., Mackay, S., Whelan, M., Hadley, B., & Kelly, K. (2020). 'You can't just take bits of my story and put them into some play': Ethical dramaturgy in the contemporary Australian performance climate. *Performing Ethos: International Journal of Ethics in Theatre & Performance,* 10 (Ethical Dramaturgies), 69–87. https://doi.org/10.1386/peet_00018_1

Saldaña, J. (2003). Dramatizing data: A primer. *Qualitative Inquiry, 9*(2), 218–236. https://doi.org/10.1177/1077800402250932

Saldaña, J. (2011). *Ethnotheatre: Research from Page to Stage.* Taylor & Francis Group. https://ebookcentral.proquest.com/lib/qut/detail.action?docID=795261

Salter, C. (2010). *Entangled: Technology and the Transformation of Performance.* The MIT Press. https://doi.org/10.7551/mitpress/9780262195881.001.0001

Tompkins, J. (2016). Editorial comment: theatre, the digital, and the analysis and documentation of performance. *Theatre Journal, 68*(4), xi–XIV. https://www.proquest.com/scholarly-journals/editorial-comment-theatre-digital-analysis/docview/1876058017/se-2?accountid=13380

2

HISTORIOGRAPHY

A summary of technology and theatre

While it is interesting to imagine the earliest examples of humanity enhancing their storytelling with technology – perhaps even millions of years ago from the moment fire was discovered – practicality demands a more truncated discussion of technology and the theatre. To my mind, it is entirely conceivable – and even inevitable – that the caveperson Grog picked up a flaming branch to enhance the reenactment of their almost-fatal mammoth-hunting adventure earlier that day. Providing their Homo erectus companion, Urgh, with the most realistic and dramatically impactful experience, the flaming wood, an early form of technology, rendered a device to shine light on the scene and create shadow play in the darkest reaches of their cave.

However, there is no way this can be verified, and I am not a historian nor an archaeologist, so I have no idea if Grog, Urgh, and mammoth even walked the earth during the same era. Partly for this reason, the examination that now follows spans the verifiable and well-trodden historical landscape known as Western theatre, from the ancient Greek adoption of stage machinery to contemporary explorations in digital and virtual realms, highlighting how these advancements have transformed the artistic and technical aspects of producing plays. This truncated historiographic summary details some of the evolutionary highlights of technological integration in theatre, focusing on key areas such as stage mechanics, lighting, sound, audiovisual projection, computer technology, augmented reality, virtual reality, and artificial intelligence. This demonstrates that AI, AR, and VR technologies are not necessarily radically new interventions in theatre and theatre design, but the latest evolutions in the longstanding and well-established tendency of theatre and live performance to adapt and adopt new technological elements as

DOI: 10.4324/9781003521907-2

part of its dramatic world-making. A notable motif throughout the historiography is the use of technology to enhance the visual effects and impact of a live performance work, inferring a natural progression for image-based enhancements, offered by the likes of AR technology, for example, to be subsumed into the dramaturgical framework and contribute to novel ways of achieving visual effects onstage.

Ancient and classical Greek and Roman theatre

Greek theatre, stretching as far back as the 6th century BCE, is credited with introducing several mechanical devices to enhance dramatic performances. Perhaps the most well-known of these inventions is the 'deus ex machina,' with a literal meaning of 'god from the machine' or 'crane.' This crane was used to lower actors playing gods onto the stage, creating a dramatic and divine intervention at the most fortuitous of moments, providing us with the contemporary understanding of the term deus ex machina: the saving of a seemingly hopeless situation by the unpredictable but timely intervention of a person or event (Chondros, 2004). Ancient Greek theatres were also technological innovations in and of themselves, designed with remarkable acoustics that could carry the voices and sounds of the stage clearly across the farthest reaches of the audience. Even by today's standards, the level of aural quality evident in an Ancient Greek theatre, without the need for additional tools of sound amplification, is remarkable (Barkas, 2019).

The Ancient Greeks are also credited as providing the theatre with early mechanisms for scene changes. The 'periaktos,' a multi-faceted prism that could be turned to present a different image to audiences, was used to indicate a change in scenery as the narrative unfolded (Özdilek & Tıbıkoğlu, 2024). A further innovation of this device was the ability for images to be changed mid-scene. While the audience was presented with one image, ancient stagehands could remove and replace the images on the hidden sides of the periaktos to initiate the next scene change. Similarly, the wheeled platform known as an 'eccyclema,' a device that came later during the period of Classical Greek theatre, could be pushed on and offstage as necessary. The eccyclema is known to have been used to house scenes within scenes, presenting an event taking place in an interior room, or to bring an offstage scene into the action (Trapido, 1949, p. 21).

Roman theatre continued to develop stage innovations after the decline of the Greek influence, incorporating increasingly complex machinery and elaborate designs. Well-known for extravagant effects – such as complex plumbing and engineering techniques that enabled the flooding of purpose-built arenas with water to facilitate the telling of maritime stories, or naumachiae (Harrison, 2015) – the Ancient Romans developed technologies that both enhanced the dramatic experience and adhered to their overall aesthetic of grandeur. The Roman concept of the 'scaenae frons' (stage front) could be seen to have led to the eventual establishment of the proscenium – and later, the proscenium arch – as the dominant design for a traditional performance space for much of Western theatre's history (Motycka Weston, 2023). The Scaenae frons was an architectural structure that was sound enough to house elaborate systems and mechanical devices to aid in the changing of scenery. With its frame-like structure, this installation likely also paved the way for the scenic backdrop, in Roman times noted for its elaborate decorations and splendid architectural design reminiscent of imperial palaces: perhaps also a very early demonstration of applying captivating visual impact to generate scenic immersion for audiences.

The trap door also emanated from the Roman stage, rendered possible due to the architectural size and strength of their theatres (Holloway, 2002). Enabling the perception of sudden appearances and disappearances, a seemingly simple hole in the stage would eventually become a standard piece of equipment in theatres centuries later, finding particular prominence in playhouses of the Victorian era (Johnson, 2007). Evidenced across the history of staged drama, from Shakespeare's Globe to the theatre companies of today, and even stadium extravaganzas headlined by the likes of Taylor Swift, the trapdoor is an ingenious piece of theatrical invention that still manages to surprise and excite audiences the world over. Particularly a surprise for frontman Chris Martin of the band Coldplay and solo artist Olivia Rodrigo, both falling through open trapdoors mid-concert at separate gigs only weeks apart during the year 2024 in Melbourne, Australia.

Medieval, renaissance, and a little Baroque theatre

The medieval period was hallmarked by the influence of the Church across Europe. Plays were almost exclusively connected with and supported by – or at least had their content approved and policed by – the religious establishment (Faedo, 1997). As the medieval period unfolded, the transition from fixed to movable stages is perhaps the most widely accepted characteristic of the era. Shifting from a larger, permanent stage to platforms on wheels – referred to as wagons – saw a necessary decline in the use of mechanical machinery to supplement and heighten the dramatic experience. While static stages remained in some form, the mobile stage, or pageant wagon, could be seen as a step away from complicated, immobile, dramatic technologies. Apart from the wagon itself, as an example of mechanical engineering, complex stage machinery gave way to codified stage designs, where specific sections of the pageant wagon platform were demarcated into separate 'loci,' often divided between heaven, earth, and hell (Young, 1967). While the use of the pageant wagon as the performance space reduced the capacity for actors and performers to take advantage of previously fixed stage technologies, it conversely enabled exposure to the theatre for larger audiences. The ability to bring the story directly to the people in a town square, a local field and other areas of human gathering not only invited a kind of democratisation for theatre audiences but also enabled the church to promote its message to the masses.

Advancing further in time to the Renaissance period, theatre's most recognised components of applied technology seem to be related to innovations in visual arts and design. In the early 1400s, Filippo Brunelleschi is credited to have rediscovered the earlier Greek and later Roman technique of linear perspective, a spatial understanding that had been lost during the medieval period (The Nelson-Atkins Museum of Art, n.d.). Later, Italian designer Sebastiano Serlio influentially published ideas about the use of linear perspective specifically for theatre design, providing detailed examples and instructions on how to use this technique of visual art to create a realistic replication of a scene location onstage (Aronson, 2023b). This example further demonstrates the theatre's ongoing attempts at adopting visual technologies to achieve a sense of immersion within the scenes of a play. Also evident in Serlio's work are stage components that are recognisable even today, such as wings, a backdrop with perspective, and masking components to hide other systems of theatrical technology.

Another Italian theatre innovator was Nicola Sabbatini, also known as a pioneer in the use of techniques of perspective to revolutionise the theatrical stage. Active during the Baroque period, Sabbatini is credited with: incorporating coloured lighting effects by placing candles behind bottles filled with dyed water; the very first 'spotlight' onstage – achieved by placing a concave mirror behind a lamp to produce the earliest known lighting effect of its kind; early techniques for the blackout effect; and the introduction of footlights (Gracie, 2022, p. 103; Penzel, 1978, p. 10). Italian staging techniques then made their way across Europe, with the father of English Architecture, Inigo Jones, recognised as bringing these innovations to Britain's playhouses in the Early Modern Era (Aronson, 2023a). Jones incorporated the techniques of perspective to achieve realistic backdrops, as well as reintroducing examples of the periaktos, experimenting with movable scenery, incorporating wings to enhance perceptions of depth, and promoting the proscenium arch as standard in English theatre architecture.

18th- and 19th-century theatre

The 18th and 19th centuries saw major technological advancements in theatre. To depart from the Euro-centric focus of this historiography for a moment, the Japanese are known to have developed the revolving stage during the late 1700s (Tsuboi, 2001). Originally designed as a component of traditional Kabuki theatre, the 回り舞台 (mawari butai) was positioned stage centre and allowed casts and entire sets to be rotated in-place, revolutionising the potential for scene changes and bringing a level of efficiency to multi-set performances, whereby audiences could be transported to entirely different dramatic locations without the interruption of a lengthy change-over. Achieving such shifts in location in full view of the audience also, no-doubt, enhanced the experience and created a level of excitement amongst onlookers, in much the same way modern audiences are titillated by the sudden transformation of a stage revolve. This technology is said to have made its way into the Western theatre tradition via what would now be considered Germany, implemented on Munich stages from the late 1800s.

Perhaps the most recognised technological developments of the 18th and 19th century stages are seen in the introduction of gas lighting. Not to be confused with the now popularised term for emotional and psychological manipulation referencing the title of the 1944 George Cukor film, newly powerful lamps literally fuelled by gas became one of the most revolutionary technologies in the development of theatrical design. Gas-powered lamps enabled the control of stage lighting to a greater level of nuance, allowing for the use of a wider range of intensities and colours (Brockett & Hildy, 2008). These developments reinforced lighting effects as a key component to enhance the dramatic experience for audiences.

The early 1800s also heralded the invention of the chemically driven 'limelight,' attributed to inventor Thomas Drummond (Gasché, 2002). A combination of calcium oxide, inflamed oxygen, and hydrogen generated a powerful yet comparably safe lighting source. Widely deployed in theatres by the 1860s, the invention of limelight in the early 19th century provided an additional technological tool alongside existing gas lighting, enabling a powerful and focused light source that could be used for spotlight effects and to more keenly provide inferences of sunlight and moonlight onstage. However, it was the advent of electric lighting in the late 19th century that led to our contemporary understanding of stage lighting. Electric lighting not only improved the safety and versatility of stage illumination, but further enhanced the ability of lighting designs and effects to deliver nuanced visual storytelling.

Pioneers, such as Adolphe Appia, a Swiss architect and lighting theorist, provided the foundations for what became standard practice in lighting for the stage, particularly for the realism genre. He has been celebrated as the most important innovator in the history of stage lighting (Beacham, 2013). Appia's 1899 work, *Die Musik und die Inszenierung*, detailed techniques for deploying lighting to: enhance the multi-dimensional aspects of the theatrical stage; act as a unifying component to draw the action and actors together;

enhance the theatrical soundscape by pairing lighting with music; and highlight actors and areas of dramatic action. Still relevant to stage lighting theory and practice, the likes of Appia were responsible for advocating for stage illumination to exist in a greater capacity than to simply improve visibility but also to enhance the emotional and psychological depth of performances (Beacham, 1993).

20th-century theatre

The 20th century brought significant changes to theatre. The introduction of microphones and amplifiers allowed actors' voices to be heard clearly in large venues. Amplified sound effects, particularly recorded sounds, became an integral part of productions as directors and designers were enabled to create more immersive and atmospheric experiences through the orchestration of soundscapes. With the advent of film craft and technology in the previous century, a new possibility for theatre makers would also emerge. As the 20th century unfolded, film and projection became increasingly common theatrical effects, adding a new visual dimension to stage performances.

Sound technology

Sound design in theatre evolved to include advanced speaker systems, wireless microphones, and digital soundboards. These technologies ensure that every nuance of the performance is heard clearly, regardless of the venue's size. These developments expanded the range of vocal and musical expression possible onstage, allowing for more complex and layered soundscapes. Sound designers also began to incorporate immersive audio techniques, such as surround sound, to create more engaging auditory experiences.

Audiovisual projection and multimedia integration

The mid-20th century witnessed the emergence of audiovisual (AV) projection as a significant technological tool in theatre. The use of film and slide projections began as a means of enhancing scenic design, offering dynamic backgrounds and visual effects that could shift the audience's perception of time and space (Aronson, 2005). In some ways, this could be considered a re-imagining of the ancient innovations such as the periaktos, but in a more scalable, adaptable form enabled by these new developments in visual technologies. As projectors and graphics programs evolved, so too did their application in theatre. High-definition projectors and, later, LED screens, are used to create stunning backdrops, interactive sets, and visual effects that enhance the storytelling experience.

By the late 20th century, digital projection was understood as a staple in avant-garde and experimental theatre, with artists like Robert Lepage and the Wooster Group integrating complex multimedia elements into their productions (Butterworth & McKinney, 2009). The integration of media in theatre led to the development of what has been termed 'mediatized performance,' where the boundaries between live action and mediated content blur, challenging notions of liveness and questioning the influence of a mediatised culture on live arts (See: Auslander, 2022). This shift also initiated some of the earliest debates about the role of technology in potentially undermining the immediacy and intimacy of live performance, a concern that continues to influence both practitioners and scholars in the field as advances in AR, VR, and AI technologies unfold. The result of these developments in digital projection and mediatised effects has been an entirely new area of theory and practice within the broader performance studies field: intermediality in performance (Bay-Cheng et al., 2010; Chapple & Kattenbelt, 2006).

Computer technology

The advent of powerful and commercially accessible computer systems in the late 20th and early 21st centuries marked a new era in the relationship between theatre and technology. Computers have enabled more sophisticated control systems for lighting, sound, and projection, allowing greater precision and synchronisation in live performance. This has led to what is labelled "responsive environments" (Salter, 2010). Examples include stage management software, such as Lightwright in the 1980s and, later, into the first decade of the 21st century, Qlab. These programmes streamline the process of cueing lights, sound, and projections and enable precise manipulation for lighting and visual effects cues. These systems enhance the level of control the creating artist has over the effects and ultimately increase the potential impact of the experience on audiences. The rise of digital theatre – performances that are either mediated through or entirely created by digital means – began with the co-opting of computer systems for dramatic performance purposes and has expanded the possibilities of what constitutes a theatrical experience (Masura, 2020a).

From the 20th into the 21st century theatre (and beyond?)

A perhaps narrowly specific, but noteworthy, development of the early 21st century is the transition from traditional incandescent lighting to LED technology. This shift has hailed significant advancements in a creative team's ability to design a theatrical experience. LED lights offer flexibility, energy efficiency, and the ability to create a wide range of colours and effects, often remotely from a lighting programme that can even be downloaded to a mobile device. The relatively low cost of effective LED lighting equipment has also brought with it an accessibility previously unknown to small and independent theatre makers in terms of access to theatrical lighting with comparably simple installation that does not necessarily require costly theatrical crews to install. Though, some would argue that LED technology cannot compare to the look and artistic feel of the effect onstage of older incandescent theatre lamps.

More broadly, the integration of digital technology and multimedia has become a feature of many examples of contemporary theatre throughout the late 20th and early 21st centuries, leveraging computer-generated imagery (CGI) and virtual environments to offer new avenues for scenic design, narrative exploration and performance dissemination. These developments have led to experimentations that have spawned an entirely new label, digital theatre, as well as expressions of VR and AR performances that challenge fundamental understandings of the live theatre form, the place of the audience and the notion of liveness. AI is also inevitably finding a space within the theatre, with applications ranging from marketing and promotion to scriptwriting and performance. AI algorithms can be used to analyse scripts, suggest edits, and even generate new content, while AI-driven characters are being developed to interact with performers and audiences.

Digital theatre

A subset of digital performance, digital theatre encompasses a broad range of practices and demonstrates a variety of proposed meanings. Perhaps the most useful summary of the wider form is provided by Jen Parker-Starbuck and Sarah Bay-Cheng, in their aptly named resource, *A Concise Introduction to Digital Performance* (2022). Broadly, it is declared that "Digital Performance encompasses the use of different media technologies in the performing arts, including theatre, dance, and other live arts" (p. 4). The authors also note the similarly broad definition of Steve Dixon, that it is "all performance works where computer technology plays a *key* role" [original emphasis] (2007, p. 3). Nadja Masura seems to place firmer limits on the form, identifying several criteria as requisites to meet the definition of digital theatre. Masura's limitations include the requirement for a co-present audience and actor occupying the same physical, shared space (2020b).

Aleksander Sasha Dundjerović offers another distinction, separating Digital Theatre – described generically as digital technology to make, represent and share live events, such as the streaming of recorded live performances on film or television – in contrast to "Live Digital Theatre" (2023).

The distinction is between the former, which is a live performance that has been digitised by recording it and then distributed through digital means, and the latter, which is a live performance that assumedly includes digital elements in its form. Dundjerović makes further allowances for more recent developments in media and technology, including the use of social media as a tool of and for performance, partly overturning Masura's requirement for co-location with an additional consideration of how the live, virtual, and physical spaces are each real environments that can themselves be considered co-located within an evolving understanding of virtual worlds. Furthermore, Matthew Causey (2016) has already explored the 'post-digital,' declaring the digital and real, mediatised and corporeal, are now indistinguishable and cannot be separated by distinction.

These definitions provide that digital theatre could span the gambit of computer-digital-technology-infused, enabled, and distributed performances that exist today. From the National Theatre's 'At Home' online streaming service, a catalogue of recorded works that emerged from the global shutdown of live theatre venues due to the COVID-19 pandemic, perhaps even stretching to elements of Tim Bird's 2012 rendition of the musical *Pippin*. Performed at London's Menier Chocolate Factory, *Pippin* included a computer-generated avatar, no doubt a *key* role in the play, sword fighting onstage with a real-life actor (Lampert-Graux, 2012). Furthermore, the advent of 'Zoom' theatre, or the synchronous, online broadcasting of theatrical scripts performed by actors via video conferencing software, with audiences logging in to sit and watch as fellow Zoomers, has also generated a newly accepted form of digital theatre (Pike et al., 2020). Borne from the response to the isolation rules of COVID-19, the impact of the global health crisis on theatre and performance and the way it forced creatives to employ digital technologies to continue to create is undeniable.

In general, constant technological developments enabling greater internet access and faster online speeds continue to support ever-evolving opportunities for digital theatre. Also considering the increasing capabilities and affordability of screens and other computer devices on a domestic level, as well as improvements in access to and the quality of CGI, enhancements in digital theatre effects are ongoing. Advances in projection and vision-effect hardware and software on a commercial scale also contribute to the enduring growth in digital theatre and the diversity of forms in which it continues to be found.

Virtual reality (VR) and augmented reality (AR)

Arguably extensions and/or components of the Digital Theatre form, AR and VR continue to find ways of incorporation into live performance, offering dramatic experiences that challenge the conventional boundaries of the stage. Briefly understood, VR "entirely overwrite[s] the visual and audio elements of a user's physical surroundings with digitally rendered content," while AR "superimpose[s] digitally rendered content onto the user's surroundings such that this content seems to inhabit the physical environs" (Hunter, 2024, p. 177). In other words, VR places the human body in the virtual environment, while AR places the virtual environment in the human world (See also: Pike, 2019). VR, then, can be seen as a natural progression of developments in immersion, lending itself to immersive experiences that entirely subsume participants in a virtual realm.

Conversely, AR can be viewed as a tool to generate effects – augmentations – atop/within the physical world of the play, in much the same way historical developments such as the periaktos, adaptation of linear perspective in stage design, and the adoption of mediated projection have done. There is also a potential crossover between VR and AR technologies and what is termed 'virtual production.' While more aligned with the film and screen arts, the incorporation of digital animations and effects through virtual or AR often requires skills associated with virtual production – animators, programmers, and digital content creators, for example. This further extends the discussion around preserving the unique qualities of theatre and live performance to distinguish AR/VR theatre from something like virtual production while adopting its techniques to enhance and improve the incorporation of related technologies in a practical way.

Virtual reality

The entirely virtual environments created by VR generally require the use of headsets or wearable devices paired with motion-tracking technology. While this enables theatrical performances to take place in fully digital spaces, allowing a level of interactivity and immersion that is different from that attainable in traditional theatre, there are also drawbacks to the form. These include artist access to and proficiency with the required technology, as well as physical barriers that influence the audience's ability to wear and use the equipment. So, while VR offers unique potentials to influence the dramatic experience, there are still important considerations to overcome when planning a piece of VR theatre.

There is also ongoing debate about the VR experience as an expression of the theatrical form overall. Distinctions between theatre, gaming and filmic encounters are often blurred. The 2019 production, *Hamlet 360: Thy Father's Spirit*, by Boston's Commonwealth Shakespeare Company, used 360° camera technology to record a new telling of Shakespeare's classic. The production was promoted as an opportunity for audiences to experience the well-known tale from a new perspective, filmed and broadcast so viewers could experience the play, through a VR headset, from the point of view of the ghost of Hamlet's dead father (Commonwealth Shakespeare Company, 2024). This prominent example of VR theatre may be seen to raise contentions around the delineation between theatre and film. The entire event is still available online, a recording of actors enacting the play that is then made available to audiences to stream online, ideally viewed using a VR headset. The provocation is often made of examples like this: is it a VR theatre experience or a VR film?

Stretching the VR as a theatre form even further, in 2019/2020 immersive experience company, Tender Claws, teamed with live events creators, Piehole, to produce the online experience, *The Under Presents*. With directing credits to Samantha Gorman and Danny Cannizzaro, the project leveraged an existing online gaming environment with audience members able to transport into this virtual realm at their leisure using their personal VR devices. Thereafter, audience members were enabled to explore the environment, interact with roving actors and enter an online performance space where scenes inspired by Shakespeare's *The Tempest* were presented synchronously (Baur, 2021). The online gaming genesis of this event is notable, the experience itself raising myriad questions about the distinction between interactive performance and interactive game, the gamification of live digital theatre, the line between audience and performer, and the distinction between dramatic narrative and ludonarrative.

Augmented reality

AR technology has a variety of applications in a live theatre context. It can be used to enhance set designs, create interactive props, generate animated characters and conjure any number of audio or visual effects. This technology is increasingly positioned as a pivotal tool in the evolution of contemporary performance, not only applied to create immersive and interactive experiences but also to enhance traditional theatrical design techniques and challenge existing notions of liveness, space, and audience engagement. However, the adoption of AR in theatre has also raised similar questions to those familiar with VR, particularly regarding accessibility and the nature of the audience experience. AR technology often requires specialised equipment, such as tablets or headsets or smartphones, which may not be accessible to all audience members. Equipment may be cost prohibitive for theatre makers to experiment with, and often requires specialist skills to work with effectively. While AR provides opportunities for the evolution of live performance, it is in a comparably nascent stage with some way to go before its application in a live theatre context may be fully understood.

Even so, Carnegie Melon University's, Arts Management and Technology Laboratory, credits Australian director, Julie Martin, as the first to incorporate AR technology into a theatrical performance, as early as 1994 (Clement,

2021). The claim is of a work titled, *Dancing in Cyberspace*, where acrobats are said to have interacted with virtual objects. Though, a group of researchers from Nanyang Technological University attribute the first use of AR in theatre to a Singapore-Canada co-production that premiered in 2007, titled *The Ultimate Commodity* and *Everyman: The Ultimate Commodity*, in each location, respectively (Jernigan et al., 2009). Upon investigation, the Singapore-Canadian claim is extensively reported by its researchers, while additional accounts verifying the content of Martin's production are yet to be located. In a more definitive example, in 2019, the RSC, in collaboration with the US firm, Magic Leap, developed an AR version of the 'Seven Ages of Man' monologue from Shakespeare's, *As You Like It* (Hunter, 2024, p. 187). Magic Leap created of a head-mounted AR device that overlays augmentations atop the wearer's physical environment, similar to the way many VR effects require a participant to wear a set of goggles. Recently, the Shanghai Theatre Academy was involved in bringing a classic Chinese Opera to the stage using AR glasses technology, merging virtual performance with physical stage settings (Hang, 2023).

While current VR technology inevitably requires a participant to use equipment for the experience – a headset, computer or some kind of screen – achieving AR effects is possible both with and without audiences/participants directly engaging with enabling devices. An additional benefit of AR-enhanced performances is that they can be experienced by an audience without the need to directly interact with/wear enabling equipment. This preserves a traditional theatre experience – particularly elements of liveness and the communal aspect of a physically co-located audience – and alleviates some of the limitations associated with costly and cumbersome kit that VR requires. In this way, AR actively blurs the line between reality and effect, presenting new possibilities to explore the notion of mixed realities. This application of AR evidences its most natural extension as an additional apparatus in the theatre-making toolkit. If embraced, it will become yet another way to enhance the live performance experience, adding augmentations into the reality (re)presented onstage, enhancing the artist's ability to bring their world to life, in the same way that painted scenery, electric lighting and immersive audio and visual tools have done. AR technology, embedded directly into/atop the physical world of the artwork without the need for additional devices adorned by an audience, is therefore seen as a natural evolution of theatrical creative expression and design.

Pioneering UK theatre company, Blast Theory, are known as early adopters of technology in their live performance practices and have been experimenting with the notion of AR, perhaps ahead of their time. In 1998, Blast Theory embarked on a series of endeavours to push beyond the binary notion of reality/AR, to explore what they termed mixed realities (Benford et al., 1998).

In a later report prepared for Sweden's Royal Institute of Technology (Benford et al., 1999), Blast Theory worked to differentiate the notion of mixed reality as an extension of forms such as AR, ultimately describing their development of a "tessellated mixed reality." This is defined as a joining-together of multiple physical and virtual spaces, exemplified in a material used by the company to set the boundary of a theatrical space, in the form of a "dry rain curtain." This curtain is a permeable boundary and allows performers, props and audiences to pass through, with the intention of enhancing the perception of being able to physically enter and exit a virtual world (Benford et al., 2002). It is noted that this experiment dates to 1998, while the Singapore-Canada collaboration above premiered in 2007. However, there is a distinction: Blast Theory's example of AR includes a 'physical' effect that can be breached by an audience to enhance the experience of the immersion – an immersive theatre experience – whereas *The Ultimate Commodity* is understood as a traditional piece of theatre incorporating computer-generated AR characters/effects.

In some ways extending upon the AV-experimentations of mediated performance works from the likes of Blast Theory, and others such as Robert Lepage and the Wooster Group, AR is increasingly employed to create immersive and interactive experiences not only by specialist makers but a range of theatre companies, allowing a growing number of audiences to engage with performances through this technology. For example, The RSC's 2016 production, *The Tempest*, has been credited as a first in mainstream/mainstage examples of incorporating a principal character, in a theatrical performance, through live motion capture technology (Borsuk, 2019). A collaboration between RSC, global tech company, Intel, and performance capture and virtual production company, The Imaginarium, director Gregory Doran's play is said to be a watershed moment for technology in theatre, bringing the character of Ariel to the stage through step-changing use of projected, real-time AR animation effects embedded within live performance.

The use of AR in theatre represents a significant development in the evolution of performance arts. While AR offers innovative possibilities for storytelling and audience engagement, similarly to other expressions of digital theatre, it also challenges established conventions of theatre and raises important questions about the nature of live performance. As theatre practitioners and scholars continue to explore the potential of AR, it is likely that this technology will play an increasing role in shaping the future of many live theatre experiences.

Artificial intelligence (AI) – And the future of theatre?

AI represents a potentially powerful frontier in the integration of technology into theatre. The term is understood to encompass computer-driven functions such as machine learning, natural language processing, and autonomous electronic systems. It has the potential to revolutionise various aspects of theatrical production, from automated lighting and sound design to the creation of AI-driven characters and narratives, with AI algorithms able to analyse scripts, suggest edits, and even generate new content. Indeed, currently, one of the most contentious examples of this technology in the creative arts is the use of AI algorithms to generate scripts or replicate the voices and physicality of real-life actors, introducing the notion of non-human agency into the creative process while also challenging traditional understandings of authorship and creativity. AI also offers potential opportunities to enhance audience engagement through analysis and assessment of target audience likes and dislikes, as well as the enhancement of immersive environments whereby it may be possible to tailor effects to the desires of individual audience members in real time.

One of the earliest instances of AI integration in live theatre is the 2016 project, *Beyond the Fence*, which is credited as the world's first AI-generated musical (Liu, 2019). Directed by Luke Sheppard and staged at London's Arts Theatre, it was produced in a collaboration between researchers at Cambridge University and the theatre company Wingspan Productions. The musical is set amongst the Greenham Common Women's Peace Camp, a woman-led movement against the placement of nuclear weapons at a British Airforce base that began in 1981 and survived in some form until the year 2000. The musical received mixed reviews, with *The Guardian* labelling it pleasant and inoffensive yet problematic in its seeming unawareness of the feminist movement it places at the core of its plot (Gardner, 2016). The inability of AI to understand and appropriately represent the complicated nuances of gender-based social and political discourse is highlighted here, further questioning the role of this emerging technology in reinforcing bias. Despite the criticisms, *Beyond the Fence* marked a significant milestone in exploring AI's potential to influence creative practice in theatre, with the process itself recorded and produced as a documentary for commercial television (Colton et al., 2022).

A further prominent example of AI used in the creation of theatre, would be the THEaiTRE project (Rosa et al., 2021). This experiment in AI and dramatic creativity is a collaboration between London's Czech Centre and Prague's Švanda Theatre, bringing together both natural language and theatre researchers. The THEaiTRE project credits its 2021 production, *AI: When a robot writes a play*, as the first theatrical play written by artificial intelligence (van Heerden et al., 2023). The AI-generated text was noted for its unexpected and sometimes surreal dialogue, which challenged the actors to engage with material that was inherently unpredictable.

Also in 2021, London's Young Vic theatre provided an early example of leveraging AI as a character within a performance. Directed by Jennifer

Tang, the pragmatically titled, *AI*, invited an audience into the creative process, recruiting GPT-3 OpenAI technology in a real-time 'conversation,' where it was prompted to discuss and develop a new play in collaboration with the human production team (Akbar, 2021). One of the most notable results of this experiment was the problematic way in which the technology seemed to inherit very human biases, inevitably as a result of its function: mining and learning from the immense data sets already created by humans. It seems that the AI in this story replicated the racial bias inherent in many aspects of Western-centric culture and public discourse, insisting on crafting a Muslim character it described as a terrorist (Perrigo, 2021).

While the use of AI in theatre is still in its nascent stages, its potential implications for the future of live theatre and performance are profound, offering new possibilities for interactivity, personalisation, and even autonomous creative processes. Furthermore, AI's ability to analyse vast amounts of data and generate narrative content based on patterns presents a new form of dramaturgy that is both collaborative and autonomous. Collaborative in that it makes assessments based on the existing datasets created by humans as well as accepts influence from human prompts to inform its output. Autonomous in the way it collects, collates and produces its responses. The incorporation of AI into theatre has also sparked debates about the potential dehumanisation of the art form. Critics may argue that while AI can enhance production efficiency and introduce novel creative elements, it may also risk reducing the emotional and empathetic qualities that are central to live theatre. AI's eventual consumption by the theatre is ultimately dependent upon people's desire for how they want their art to be and the kind of performances humans actually want to make and see (Eacho, 2023). The ethical implications of using AI in theatre, particularly regarding the replacement of human labour and the commodification of creative processes, remain critical concerns for practitioners, scholars, and audiences.

A conclusion (but not the end of theatre history!)

This concise historiography of technology in live theatre reveals an ever-evolving relationship that has continually influenced how the art form tells stories. From ancient mechanics that manipulated scene and setting, to gas and electric innovations in lighting and sound, and contemporary computer-powered explorations of AR, VR, and AI, technology has expanded the possibilities of what can be achieved in live performance and how dramatic narratives may be brought to life onstage. While any developments may be met with both enthusiasm and scepticism, the historical reality and latent potentiality infer an undeniable enrichment of the theatrical landscape, offering new tools for artistic expression and audience engagement.

As technology continues to evolve, so too will its impact on theatre, challenging practitioners and scholars alike to reconsider the boundaries of the medium and the nature of live theatre and performance itself.

References

Akbar, A. (2021). Rise of the Robo-Drama: Young Vic creates new play using artificial intelligence. *The Guardian*. https://www.theguardian.com/stage/2021/aug/24/rise-of-the-robo-drama-young-vic-creates-new-play-using-artificial-intelligence

Aronson, A. (2005). *Looking into the Abyss: Essays on Scenography*. University of Michigan Press. https://doi.org/10.3998/mpub.22239

Aronson, A. (2023a). Inigo Jones (1573–1652). In *Fifty Key Theatre Designers*. Taylor & Francis Group. https://ebookcentral.proquest.com/lib/qut/detail.action?docID=30760930

Aronson, A. (2023b). Sebastiano Serlio (1475– 1554[?]). In *Fifty Key Theatre Designers* (pp. 13–19). Taylor & Francis Group. https://ebookcentral.proquest.com/lib/qut/detail.action?docID=30760930

Auslander, P. (2022). *Liveness: Performance in a Mediatized Culture*. Taylor & Francis Group. https://ebookcentral.proquest.com/lib/qut/detail.action?docID=7127484

Barkas, N. (2019). The contribution of the stage design to the acoustics of ancient greek theatres. *Acoustics*, *1*(1), 337–353. https://www.mdpi.com/2624-599X/1/1/18

Baur, D. (2021). The under presents by Samantha Gorman and Danny Cannizzaro (review). *Theatre Journal*, *73*(1), 106–108. https://www.proquest.com/schol2?arly-journ2?als/i-under-presents-s2?am2?anth2?a-gorm2?an-d2?anny-c2?annizz2?aro/docview/2507716335/se-2?2?accountid=13380

Bay-Cheng, S., Kattenbelt, C., Lavender, A., & Nelson, R. (2010). *Mapping Intermediality in Performance*. Amsterdam University Press. https://ebookcentral.proquest.com/lib/qut/detail.action?docID=564063

Beacham, R. C. (1993). *Adolphe Appia: Texts on Theatre* (1st ed.). Routledge. https://doi.org/10.4324/9781315002972

Beacham, R. C. (2013). *Adolphe Appia: Artist and Visionary of the Modern Theatre* (1st edition. ed., Vol. 6). Routledge. https://doi.org/10.4324/9781315077284

Benford, S., Fraser, M., Reynard, G., Koleva, B., & Drozd, A. (2002). *Staging and Evaluating Public Performances as an Approach to CVE Research*. The 4th International Conference on Collaborative Virtual Environments, Bonn, Germany. https://doi.org/10.1145/571878.571891

Benford, S., Greenhalgh, C., Reynard, G., Brown, C., & Koleva, B. (1998). Understanding and constructing shared spaces with mixed-reality boundaries. *ACM Transactions on Computer-Human Interaction (TOCHI)*, *5*(3), 185–223. https://doi.org/10.1145/292834.292836

Benford, S., Norman, S. J., Bowers, J., Adams, M., Row-Farr, J., Koleva, B., Taylor, I., Rinman, M.-L., Martin, K., Schnädelbach, H., & Greenhalgh, C. (1999). *Pushing Mixed Reality Boundaries*. Centre for User Oriented IT Design. https://www.blasttheory.co.uk/wp-content/uploads/1999/02/1999-research_pushing_mixed_reality_boundaries.pdf

Borsuk, A. (2019). Innovating Shakespeare: The politics of technological partnership in the royal Shakespeare company's the tempest (2016). *Humanities*, *8*(1), 42. https://doi.org/10.3390/h8010042

Brockett, O. G., & Hildy, F. J. (2008). *History of the Theatre* (10th ed.). Pearson.

Butterworth, P., & McKinney, J. (2009). *The Cambridge Introduction to Scenography*. Cambridge University Press. https://search.alexanderstreet.com/view/work/bibliographic_entity%7Cbibliographic_details%7C3516886

Causey, M. (2016). Postdigital performance. *Theatre Journal, 68*(3), 427–441. https://www.jstor.org/stable/26367339

Chapple, F., & Kattenbelt, C. (2006). *Intermediality in Theatre and Performance*. Brill. https://ebookcentral.proquest.com/lib/qut/detail.action?docID=6914018

Chondros, T. G. (2004). "Deus-Ex-Machina" Reconstruction and Dynamics. *International Symposium on History of Machines and Mechanisms*, Dordrecht.

Clement, K. (2021). *What is Augmented Reality?* Carnegie Mellon University. Retrieved 11 September 2024 from https://amt-lab.org/blog/2021/8/using-augmented-reality-in-classical-music

Colton, S., Llano, M. T., Hepworth, R., Charnley, J., Gale, C. V., Baron, A., Pachet, F., Roy, P., Gervas, P., Collins, N., Sturm, B., Tillman, W., Wolff, D., & Lloyd, J. R. (2022). *The Beyond the Fence Musical and Computer Says Show Documentary* Ithaca. Retrieved from https://www.proquest.com/working-papers/beyond-fence-musical-computer-says-show/docview/2674149085/se-2

Commonwealth Shakespeare Company. (2024). *Hamlet 360: Thy Father's Spirit.* Commonwealth Shakespeare Company. Retrieved 11 September 2024 from https://commshakes.org/production/hamlet-360-thy-fathers-spirit/

Dixon, S. (2007). *Digital Performance: A History of New Media in Theater, Dance, Performance Art, and Installation*. MIT Press. https://ebookcentral.proquest.com/lib/qut/detail.action?docID=3338680

Dundjerović, A. S. (2023). *Live Digital Theatre: Interdisciplinary Performative Pedagogies*. Taylor & Francis Group. https://ebookcentral.proquest.com/lib/qut/detail.action?docID=7222311

Eacho, D. (2023). Performativity without theatricality: experiments at the limit of staging AI. *Theatre and Performance Design, 9*(1–2), 20–36. https://doi.org/10.1080/23322551.2023.2210989

Faedo, M. J. Á. (1997). The role of the church in the incipient medieval drama: from street theatre to morality plays. *Selim, 7*(1), 181–192. https://doi.org/10.17811/selim.7.1997.181-192

Gardner, L. (2016, February 29). Beyond the fence review – Computer-created show is sweetly bland. *The Guardian*. https://www.theguardian.com/stage/2016/feb/28/beyond-the-fence-review-computer-created-musical-arts-theatre-london#:~:text=Arts%20theatre%2C%20London&text=Even%20when%20humans%20curate%20it,because%20that's%20where%20it's%20set

Gasché, R. (2002). Theatrum theoreticum. In T. Rajan & M. O'Driscoll (Eds.), *After Poststructuralism: Writing the Intellectual History of Theory*. University of Toronto Press. https://ebookcentral.proquest.com/lib/qut/detail.action?docID=4671172

Gracie, S. B. (2022). *Light, Dark, and the Electromagnetic Spectrum*. Tellwell Talent.

Hang, L. (2023, October 12). New tech used to promote exceptional traditional culture: China's top 10 digital innovations announced. *Global Times*. https://www.globaltimes.cn/page/202310/1299767.shtml

Harrison, G. W. M. (2015). A day at the races theatre: The spectacle of performance in the Roman Empire. In G. W. M. Harrison (Ed.), *Brill's Companion to Roman Tragedy*. Brill. https://ebookcentral.proquest.com/lib/qut/detail.action?docID=2144880

Holloway, J. (2002). Theatre types. In *Illustrated Theatre Production Guide* (pp. 13–18). Routledge. https://doi.org/10.4324/9780080491516-6

Hunter, E. B. (2024). Augmented reality and theatre. *Theatre Journal, 76*(2), 177–195. https://doi.org/10.1353/tj.2024.a932167

Jernigan, D., Fernandez, S., Pensyl, R., & Shangping, L. (2009). Digitally augmented reality characters in live theatre performances. *International Journal of Performance Arts and Digital Media, 5*(1), 35–49. https://doi.org/10.1386/padm.5.1.35_1

Johnson, R. (2007). Tricks, traps and transformations. *Early Popular Visual Culture, 5*(2), 151–165. https://doi.org/10.1080/17460650701433673

Lampert-Graux, E. (2012). Tim bird's video-infused vision for pippin. *Live Design (Online)*. https://www.proquest.com/trade-journals/tim-birds-video-infused-vision-pippin/docview/919210794/se-2?accountid=13380

Liu, S. (2019). Everybody's song making. *Performance Research, 24*(1), 120–128. https://doi.org/10.1080/13528165.2019.1594267

Masura, N. (2020a). *Digital Theatre: The Making and Meaning of Live Mediated Performance, US & UK 1990–2020*. Palgrave Macmillan. https://doi.org/10.1007/978-3-030-55628-0

Masura, N. (2020b). Introduction. In *Digital Theatre: The Making and Meaning of Live Mediated Performance, US & UK 1990–2020* (pp. 1–13). Springer International Publishing. https://doi.org/10.1007/978-3-030-55628-0_1

Motycka Weston, D. (2023). Roman Theatre's Scaenae Frons as a Thematic Edifice. In L. Landrum & S. Ridgway (Eds.), *Theatres of Architectural Imagination* (1st ed., pp. 97–108). Routledge. https://doi.org/10.4324/978 1003297666-11

Özdilek, B., & Tıbıkoğlu, H. O. (2024). New Observations on the Dionysian Scene Mosaic Panels in the House of the Triumph of Dionysus in Daphne-Antiocheia: Iconographic Description of the Periaktos System in the Decorative Architecture of the Theatre Stage Building. *Journal of Mosaic Research* (17), 119–132. https://doi.org/10.26658/jmr.1564697

Parker-Starbuck, J., & Bay-Cheng, S. (2022). *A Concise Introduction to Digital Performance: Guide*. Digital Theatre +. https://edu.digitaltheatreplus.com/content/guides/a-concise-introduction-to-digital-performance

Penzel, F. (1978). *Theatre Lighting Before Electricity*. Wesleyan University Press. https://doi.org/10.1353/book.77792

Perrigo, B. (2021, August 23). An Artificial Intelligence Helped Write This Play. It May Contain Racism. *TIME*. https://time.com/6092078/artificial-intelligence-play/

Pike, S. (2019). "Make it so ": Communal augmented reality and the future of theatre and performance. *Fusion Journal* (15), 108–118. https://doi.org/10.3316/informit.975162255148822

Pike, S., Neideck, J., & Kelly, K. (2020). 'I will teach you in a room, I will teach you now on Zoom … ': a contemporary expression of zooming by three practitioner/academics in the creative arts, developed through the spirit of the surrealist's exquisite corpse. *International Journal of Performance Arts and Digital Media, 16*(3), 290–305. https://doi.org/10.1080/14794713.2020.1822048

Rosa, R., Musil, T., Dušek, O., Jurko, D., Schmidtová, P., Mareček, D., Bojar, O., Kocmi, T., Hrbek, D., Košťák, D., Kinská, M., Nováková, M., Doležal, J., Vosecká, K., Studeník, T., & Žabka, P. (2021). *THEaiTRE 1e.0: Interactive generation of theatre play scripts*. Ithaca. https://www.proquest.com/working-papers/theaitre-1-0-interactive-generation-theatre-play/docview/2490850571/se-2

Salter, C. (2010). *Eentangled: Technology and the Transformation of Performance*. The MIT Press. https://doi.org/10.7551/mitpress/9780262195881.001.0001

The Nelson-Atkins Museum of Art. (n.d.) *Gaining Perspective*. Retrieved 11 September 2024 from https://nelson-atkins.org/gates/gaining-perspective.html

Trapido, J. (1949). The language of the theatre: I. The greeks and romans. *Educational Theatre Journal*, *1*(1), 18–26. https://doi.org/10.2307/3204106

Tsuboi, U. (2001). Historical development of slewing rim bearing systems based on supporting mechanism of revolving stage of theatres. *Journal of Japanese Society of Tribologists*, *46*(11), 836–841.

van Heerden, I., Duman, Ç., & Bas, A. (2023). Performing the post-anthropocene: AI: When a robot writes a play. *TDR: The Drama Review*, *67*(4), 104–120. https://doi.org/10.1017/S1054204323000448

Young, M. J. (1967). The york pageant wagon. *Communications Monographs*, *34*(1), 1–20. https://doi.org/10.1080/03637756709375515

3

CASE STUDY 1: AR THEATRE IN AUSTRALIA

Alex: A play with holograms (The Underworld Downunder)

My journey into AR technology in live performance is rooted in a childhood fascination with Gene Roddenberry's *Star Trek*, particularly the concept of the 'Holodeck.' First introduced in the 1970s animated series and later popularised in *The Next Generation*, the Holodeck became a pivotal narrative device, allowing for limitless settings aboard a starship. This innovation addressed the narrative constraints of a static location, potentially offering a dynamic solution to audience fatigue from repetitive ship-based dramas or veiled attempts at location shifts through 'away missions.' As a theatre maker, the Holodeck's most complicating feature is the interactivity it enables between computer-generated characters and 'real' Starfleet officers. This interactivity contrasts sharply with the passive experience of traditional theatre audiences, who engage with the narrative as empathetic observers rather than active participants. It is my aim to synthesise these two elements into a new kind of theatre experience, drawing upon the realistic and real-world augmenting effects of something like the Holodeck, while preserving the traditional theatrical encounter, core to which is the notion of liveness and the shared experience of the audience, without adopting the complicating factor of audience interactivity. The decision to resist an interactive experience is merely a personal one, as a theatregoer myself, favouring a more traditional theatre encounter.

Combining AR concepts, hologram tech, and traditional theatre practices offers new opportunities for developing how we tell stories and portray characters onstage. This chapter presents the case study of *Alex: A Play with Holograms* (*Alex*), an experimental theatrical production exploring the intersection of traditional commercial theatre and augmented reality technology.

DOI: 10.4324/9781003521907-3

The play used holo-effects to generate AR components that (re)presented characters and other visual elements of the dramatic world. The discussion encompasses the motivations behind the project and some of the challenges encountered during its execution; while also frequently reflecting on aspects of the practical, artistic, and ethical considerations of utilising this emerging technology within a dramatic work.

For the sake of transparency and clarity, it should also be disclosed that I am the writer of both this book and of the play *Alex*. I also directed the world premiere production of the work, which is the focus of this chapter. This provides a deep level of understanding and engagement with the play that hopefully strengthens the discourse. As someone with experience with reflective creative practice and ethnographic research, which includes auto-ethnographic methodological inquiry, I hope that an appropriate level of criticality and analytical detachment is also demonstrable where appropriate.

Alex premiered in July, 2023, at La Boite Theatre Company in Brisbane, Australia. La Boite is Australia's oldest continuously running theatre company (*Australia's Oldest Boldest Theatre*, 2024), making it a noteworthy cultural institution in the Australian theatre context. Initially, the significance of the performance venue sat well alongside the significance of the production, the work itself a world-first incorporation of a specific kind of AR technology embedded within a theatrical play: the country's oldest theatre company hosting some of the world's newest theatrical tech. However, as this chapter touches upon, the traditional theatre practices and design of this established and prominent venue in some ways became challenges for the production, working against its complete success.

From the outset, the play was written purposefully to include AR elements within its dramaturgical design. The intention was to ensure that the inclusion of the technology was inextricable from the work, embedded within the narrative as opposed to layered atop an existing script or introduced at the stage of treatment/set and effects design. The work was also written as a commercial script, intended to appeal to a general public audience and generate interest and ticket sales, as would be required by any production in a commercial theatre venue. I make this point, as it did influence the development of the script, which would be crafted in such a way that it could later be published and reproduced by other artists and production companies if it were successful.

Therefore, in theory the script was an AR-embedded narrative, but in practice it appears as any other theatre script may, with the AR effects mentioned but not necessarily described in any special fashion with reference to how they should be reproduced, meaning that in practice they could be replicated/achieved/interpreted by any means of theatrical effect and not only by virtue of AR technologies. While some may consider this a moot point – if there is nothing 'special' about the script and embedding AR, then what is the point of embedding the AR or labelling it an AR-embedded script? – it can also be argued that this supports the underlying intention of the project team: that AR technology can and should be seen as a natural extension of theatrical expression. The result is that the AR elements can be envisioned and included in the same way and with the same sense of acceptance as a lighting and/or set designer would interpret a scene or setting description, either as the author intended or in a way that reflects their own creative interpretation, or both. The notable difference in this example is that those effects and descriptions were crafted in the writer's mind with the specific objective that they would be expressed through AR, despite the consideration that they may also be achievable through other means.

The main AR element was the title character, Alex. This character was intended to be an animated devil-like creature, serving a dual purpose as an obvious antagonist as well as a representation of the protagonist's inner demons and critical voice. For this work, the character, Alex, was operated in real-time by a physical theatre performer, placed backstage and manipulating the animated character using a motion capture system. This actor also voiced Alex, their vocals heightened with a filter effect to further enhance their devilish characteristics. Operating Alex this way was an attempt to preserve the 'liveness' of the theatre experience not just for the audience but also for the actors, enabling organic interactions between the live actors and the animated character as its operating performer adjusted and responded to their co-star's offers as the play unfolded. This method also contrasts with other techniques of including digital characters, such as pre-programmed animations, for example, which arguably lack the spontaneity and responsiveness of live performance but demand the live action to unravel with pre-determined timing that accommodates the pre-prepared recordings.

The play follows a well-tested but effective structure: the hero's journey. To provide a plot summary, the main character, a child named Charlie, is picnicking with their father to celebrate a birthday. Their dog, Egbert, is also with them. The father is abducted by the evil demon character, Alex, and taken to a hellish underworld. Charlie finds the courage to accept the quest to follow them into the underworld, find the father and bring him back, encountering friends and foes along the way. Ultimately, it is a journey of Charlie overcoming their own inner demons, climaxing in the defeat of Alex in a high-stakes dance battle. The father and child return to a changed world, their relationship strengthened with a new level of understanding between them, and Charlie with a new confidence and strength of character to navigate the challenges of their contemporary life. The pronoun pundits may notice Charlie is referred to in gender neutral terms, as the character was written without the requirement to be played by an actor with any specific gender identification. This is not a point relevant to the technology discussion of the production, but it is necessary for the underlying social and cultural intentions of the play. It is also worth noting simply to acknowledge any would-be editorial pedants reading this, who may remain enamoured of ageing grammatical conventions and demand an answer for the lack of he/she in this plot summary.

The hero's journey narrative structure was chosen quite deliberately. As a proven framework for storytelling, the consideration was that it would lend itself to audience familiarity and acceptance. Therefore, the creative team could focus on incorporating the AR elements and researchers then attempt to assess the audience's tolerance of those elements without having to focus on a potentially supplementary consideration of whether that acceptance was being overly influenced by the story structure/style. The hero's journey is known to audiences and still arguably enjoyed – or at least accepted – by most people. With this as a foundation, the hope was that the impact of the AR on an audience and how they received the narrative via AR characters and effects would be discernible, without additional focus on considering whether a post-narrative piece of mediated theatre, for example, might have influenced their experience. It is also useful to note that the creative team was a mix of practitioner-researchers from the Queensland University of Technology (QUT), contracted technologists and engineers from local AR experience companies, as well as full-time professional artists and theatre administrators – actors, designers, stage/production management, and producers.

Producing *Alex* required collaboration between immersive experience technicians, animation experts, traditional theatre technicians, performers, and a creative team including: a writer, director, dramaturg, choreographer, and audience researcher with a background in digital scenography. As becomes clear, despite the best intentions of all involved, challenges arose when deploying the AR technology as an integral component of the play, exacerbated by the differing expectations and capabilities of the creative and technical teams. The conclusion: unfortunately, the tensions between the needs of the technology to achieve the desired vision and the actual reality of a traditional theatre venue unfamiliar with AR technology impacted the overall success of the production in reaching its full potential. If AR is to become a further tool to enhance the theatrical experience, as a natural extension of the form's desire to assimilate technologies that enrich its world-making potential, then this is an example of one tension that must be overcome. Any new way of working requires some adaption of existing practices and infrastructure, just as the advent of electric lighting and sound amplification required existing theatres to install electric cables and wiring and increased the amount of time dedicated to a 'tech run' to practice additional cues. A widespread adoption of AR also requires investments and adjustments.

Alex was billed as a children's theatre performance. Advertised as an all-ages event, the show included warnings of mild horror and supernatural themes, loud noises and references to online bullying and social media. From the outset, there were concerns amongst the cast that the animated AR effects, particularly the AR character, Alex, may exacerbate any potential 'scary' impact on younger audience members. The consideration is that, rather than if they had been portrayed by actors or puppets, for example, their presentation as animations may be more likely to cause concern for much younger children. There was no data gathered to support this consideration; it was arrived at entirely through subjective discussions amongst the creative team who had children of their own. Based on lived parental experience, ages 6–12 years old and their caregivers were considered most appropriate as a target audience. As far as the project's team could distinguish, this was the first time this specific kind of motion-capture enabled AR system had been deployed to present a piece of theatre for young people in this context.

AR characters v AR effects

While the character of Alex is the main element of augmentation within the script, other AR effects included in the premiere production of the work were: a representation of the pet dog, Egbert, who helps Charlie defeat the demon; a smoke effect to enhance and mask the sudden appearance and disappearance of support characters played by real-life actors; a pickle-whirlwind to whisk-away the characters/real actors; a forest landscape and map-effect to demonstrate forward motion and the unfolding of Charlie's quest; and the all-important portal, a gateway to the underworld that enables Charlie to enter and then return from Alex's hellscape. Overall, the AR elements could then be divided into two categories: AR characters (Alex) and AR effects (the dog, smoke and pickle-wind, for example). While the AR characters can also be considered an effect, it is arguable that this division is clear enough to discern between those elements that are functional characters in the story – the AR characters – and those that provide a special effect – the AR effects.

As a further consideration of dividing AR elements of a theatrical production into the binary, character and effect, there is also the potential for the dog animation to be considered a character if a looser definition of what a character may be is adopted. While Egbert the dog did prove pivotal to the plot and dramatic action, for the purposes of this study, Egbert exists more as a device – the same way Chekhov's gun is pivotal but not played by an actor. In this respect, an animated dog can be easily categorised as an effect in favour of a non-human character, even though it may have characteristics of a character. When writing the play, Egbert was conceived to operate as an effect although pivotal to the contrivance of the plot.

This attempt at categorisation is also a way to demonstrate one of the emerging tensions that AR technology presents to live theatre: what is the place of the actor/performer, and how can, and should, this technology be deployed when considering actors of the future? Using the technology for effects is one consideration; replacing an onstage, embodied actor with an AR hologram arguably entails an entirely different set of creative, practical, moral, and ethical considerations. In the case of *Alex*, even though Egbert was decidedly an animated effect, I chose to employ an actor to provide the 'voice' of the dog live from a microphone installed backstage, at least assuaging some of my concerns about replacing the real with the digital, but also to enable a more flexible provision of the barks, yelps, and growls. The actor could adjust and provide the sound effects in time with the shifting action onstage each night, in tune with the live actors and audience, rather than relying on timed sound effect cues.

Ethics/implications of AR effects and characters

On one hand, the use of the technology to generate the visual effects used in *Alex*, such as whirlwinds, landscapes with a three-dimensional appearance and magical portals, may not be so contentious. These elements can be considered analogous to employing more traditional theatre effect mechanisms, such as scenic drops or traditional video projection. However, the incorporation of a digitally projected character such as Alex presents more nuanced considerations around substituting physical bodies onstage with animated representations. This raises concerns about replacing human actors with digital renderings as well as highlighting issues with the inherent liveness of theatre and the audience's desire for human interaction and representation onstage. The provocation arises: is there a reality where all characters become effects, represented and portrayed by animations and computers alone, replacing the human actor in totality? One answer to this possibility is found in the very core of human existence – the need and want to create.

While there is a definite prospect of a world where the completely non-human creation of characters and stories is generated by artificial intelligence alone, for example, and their subsequent performance onstage is achieved entirely through AR means, this eventuality is hardly a fait accompli. One consideration is whether, and to what extent, audiences will accept and desire the digital to replace the human in the theatrical art that they consume. In the case of *Alex*, one of the key considerations was ensuring any humanoid animations – such as the devil – could accurately reproduce the physical movements and expressions of a real-life human, otherwise, audience buy-in was lost, and empathy for the characters disappeared.

With current technology, it may simply be easier and swifter to use real actors in appropriately fantastic costumes and make-up in the first place, as we know audiences will accept and relate to them and their story.

Audience acceptance of AR characters should also be considered alongside their desire to see computer-generated augmentations as well as the artist's desire to work with the technology. While people want to create and tell and perform stories themselves, people will create and tell and perform stories themselves. The level to which they recruit technologies available to them to do that will likely vary case by case, with each creative adopting or dismissing the digital future as is appropriate to achieving the creative vision at hand. Theatre makers, and artists more generally, have always operated in this way, discerning and deciding how they will create as a natural expression of their poetic free will. There is, of course, an argument that their choice of expression is limited by the potential audience for that choice – is it theatre at all if there is no one in the audience to see it? Yet the counter consideration is that if it is interesting to the maker, then it will inevitably be interesting to someone else, even if it is only the artist's mum in the audience. Admittedly, questions of scalability and commercial success are important considerations but debatably separate from the point about artistic desire and choice.

Perhaps the profit-driven theatre companies of the world may decide it is eventually cheaper to replicate the voices and images of human actors through AR systems, subsequently using digitisations to populate their plays and replace designers of all kinds with AI rendering programmes. There is also a cultural preservation and archival element to this possibility, with the ability to 360° video record a production, or even digitally regenerate a watershed performance otherwise lost to time through AI-powered deep-fake technology resurrecting deceased stars. These replications then 'holo-grammed' onstage to reproduce the original production without the need for living performers. Questions then arise around the classification of such an eventuality as a live theatrical experience, or whether it might more likely be a filmic encounter. Though, a more positive suspicion is of a reality that is a mix of the old ways and the new. Some creative and technical roles will be replaced, others will not, and others still will evolve: the visual effects designer becoming a digital 'visioniser,' or some such thing, responsible for prompting a theatre-specific AI computer program to develop effect animations to enhance the dramatic world. Progress and change for theatre are inevitable; it has always been thus, and the theatre has always adapted and survived because people want to write stories, and people want to produce, perform, and watch stories. The play, *Alex*, stands as an example of how AR elements can enhance or at least support the performance of a physically present human actor rather than replace them.

"We have the technology. We have the capability to make ... [a holographic] ...man": The technology we used

The play achieved an AR experience using high-powered projection – at least 20k lumens – high-definition animations – created using gaming software *Unreal Engine* – Hologauze hung within the stage design and motion capture (MoCap) technology. The MoCap was a bespoke setup including a modified commercially available gaming capture system. The MoCap to animation to projection data travels through several devices, including HDBaseT extenders, HyperDeck Studios and Blackmagic MicroRecorders. The character, Alex, was operated by a physical theatre performer positioned backstage in front of the MoCap device, accompanied by an OLED screen showing a live feed of the stage. The screen was provided so that the performer was aware of all onstage action, including how their own movements appeared in the holographic projection.

While the AR effect is created on a component called Hologauze, which is a registered trademark for the particular product used in *Alex*, and this discussion adopts the term hologram to identify and describe the visual effect, the reality is a fake kind of hologram that gives the impression of a three-dimensional holo-image. In fact, the effect is achieved by casting an image onto a two-dimensional screen, albeit invisible to the naked eye under controlled lighting conditions, from a powerful but otherwise standard projector. This impression of a holographic entity continues a long history of theatrical trickery, where disparate elements are contrived in such a way as to provide an effect that appears to be one thing, but is quite another. While Hologauze was used for this project, there are no doubt other commercially available products that could also achieve the desired effect.

The holographic gauze appears invisible to the naked eye and allows complete transparency to see behind/through it but captures any images that are projected onto it. It is a fine mesh, when applied in a theatrical sense, much like a scrim or drop, finished with a sorcerer's blend of metallic coating that, when lit correctly, renders it invisible but able to capture and reflect projected images. The result is images that it captures appear as if from nowhere, providing the hologram effect. The reality is much like a regular projection screen, but the illusion is a three-dimensional image that materialises independently within the physical world around it. The result allows for animations or digital renderings of images to be projected as independent elements alongside the real-life bodies of actors and physical set/stage pieces. A most pertinent simile to describe the effect is perhaps the 1988 cult-classic film, *Roger Rabbit*, with its revolutionary combination of live action alongside animation. Instead of achieving the effect on film, however, the deployment of this kind of holographic screen to achieve an

AR experience generates a similar animated-alongside-physically-embodied effect but in a live theatre context. It is Roger Rabbit in real life.

The impression of a hologram using the techniques employed in *Alex* in some ways is simply an alternative to the well-established theatrical illusion of Pepper's Ghost. A main benefit of using the 'hologram' effect of *Alex* in favour of a Pepper's Ghost illusion, however, is the capacity for movement. Where Pepper's Ghost may require a device of containment to reflect an image, that device may be fixed or limited in movement to achieve the reflection effect. For *Alex*, the gauze covered the stage from left to right, enabling the AR characters and effects to move across the entire field of the play, to wherever the projector lens could reach. Perhaps ironically, though, the downside is that the Hologauze ran the entire width of the stage, creating an invisible barrier for the physical actors. So, while Alex was able to traverse the stage, left and right, down and up (by altering the depth and perspective of the projected image), the physical actors were limited to only the space upstage of the gauze. This demanded some considered problem solving from actors, director, and choreographer when blocking, ensuring that the onstage performances gave the impression of a full range of stage movement without ever distracting the audience by making them aware the space for onstage action and motion was limited.

Compared to alternative methods of delivering an AR experience, such as AR headsets that must be worn or smart devices that must be held up in front of the user's field of vision, the effects of *Alex* may be considered a type of mixed reality encounter. The term mixed reality lacks a consensus definition (Speicher et al., 2019) and is often used interchangeably with extended reality (Bourdot et al., 2021). In this example, the augmentations appear to be inhabiting the real world, mixing the living with the digital, without the audience being actively made aware of how the illusion is being achieved. This is contrary to being overlaid by a device in a process the audience is conscious of by virtue of their awareness of the enabling equipment. Compared to headsets and handheld devices, using a holographic gauze to display animated augmentations as part of the larger scenography preserves the shared audience experience. Removing the need for an additional device and rendering the augmentation directly onto the stage, visible to the naked eye, ensures the experience is the same as that of a traditional theatre show. Some may argue that entering a digital world through a smart device can also be a shared experience, particularly in instances where individuals' digital avatars gather in the same digital space where their controlling humans are otherwise geographically disparate. However, there is a distinction between an event that brings disparate audiences together in a digital space, and that which brings digital augmentations to an audience in a shared, physical space. *Alex* is the latter.

Take you riding in my CAR: Communal augmented reality in theatre

The type of mixed-reality event exemplified by *Alex*, enabling the shared audience experience of AR effects in a physical space, as opposed to each person encountering the augmentation via a headset or an individual screen, can be considered an example of Communal Augmented Reality, or 'CAR' (Pike, 2019). This is not a term I have invented, yet I have not been able to relocate the inciting person nor the place from which it first emerged. It is a communal experience because the audience shares the same space and time as the augmentation and witnesses it collectively in the same way they would encounter the puppets of *Avenue Q*, for example. The core offering of the theatrical experience as a communal event is preserved, and the isolation or disconnection that can result from shuttering off the outside world after donning a wearable device, for instance, is avoided. The main point of distinction between a CAR experience and other forms of AR is that it does not require audiences/users/participants to operate a device – mobile or wearable – to experience the augmentations.

As the visual effects in *Alex* are achieved by virtue of projection onto a specialist piece of gauze, anyone with the sense of sight can see and experience the augmentation as if they were watching a traditional piece of theatre. This provides the 'communal' component of the form, an audience sharing the experience as they would sitting in an auditorium for any play. Contrast this with the requirement to hold and view a scene through a smartphone via an AR app or having to wear an AR headset. Each of these device-enabled scenarios arguably takes the audience member's focus out of the communal theatre experience and draws them into the virtual world of the device, or in the case of wearable goggles, completely separates them from their fellow audience members by immersing their sense of vision, at least, within an AR headset.

The preservation of the communal experience inherent in theatre was achieved in *Alex* by creating an AR event for a live audience incorporating the holographic, augmented elements of the work alongside the real-life actors and staging that are characteristic of a traditional theatrical experience. In developing the play, the use of wearable or smart devices to generate AR effects was deliberately avoided. Instead, animations were projected onto Hologauze within the performance space, maintaining the traditional theatre experience to the greatest extent possible while incorporating digital augmentations. This approach, termed CAR, integrates digital elements into the tangible environment, preserving the shared audience experience.

CAR is not exclusive to theatre. Indeed, there are examples of holographic zoos filled with virtual animals (Mercer, 2023), and holographic concert halls, such as Seoul's "K-Live Dongdaemun," designed specifically to deliver performances by animated renderings of real-life Korean popstars to scores of music-loving audiences (Chang & Shin, 2019). Each of these examples provides the requisite communal indicators of CAR for an audience to share the same physical space and moment in time. The main difference between a theatrical performance such as *Alex*, and holographic zoos or South Korean pop holo-concerts is the liveness element of the holographic augmentation. While *Alex* demanded a live manipulation of the holographic character, holo-zoos, and concerts, are generally delivered with pre-recorded visualisations that are left to play for audiences, akin to viewing a kind of holographic film or installation. With this in mind, *Alex* can also be considered, what I have coined, a CARL experience. That is: Communal Augmented Reality – Live.

CARL: Communal augmented reality – Live

Liveness extends the 'CAR' form when considering the theatre and performance context. The element of liveness desired for *Alex* works to further enhance the communal experience, ensuring audiences and actors share in the same unique encounter each time it is performed, though their individual understanding and reaction may also be unique to them. This is a central component of the theatrical event, with liveness considered by many a defining element of theatre and a critical factor for audience experience, acknowledging the debate around its meaning is also pivotal to discussions around technology and theatre (Auslander, 2022; Meyer-Dinkgräfe, 2015; Phelan, 1993). Regardless of how it has been impacted and redefined by more recent developments in technology and the associated mediatisation and virtualisation of different elements of the theatrical form, the notion of liveness remains a critical component of a theatrical encounter (Rosvally & Sherman, 2023). CARL, then, offers the most potential for AR technology to evolve the theatrical experience.

CARL and considerations of accessibility

Another consideration of CARL is the opportunities it affords in relation to accessibility, particularly considering physical abilities, age, and economic factors. A known barrier to participating in AR experiences is access to devices, such as wearables and smart screens, as well as broader considerations of disparity in digital skills and knowledge and socio-technical and organisational resources for both audiences and artists (Brilli et al., 2023). Audiences may not have the resources or support to access or supply their own devices with the required and up-to-date hardware and software. Further, artists and arts companies may not have the resources to supply this equipment to audiences, particularly independent theatre makers.

There are also physical barriers to participating with such technologies, the literal weight of a headset or handset rendering it difficult for some to wear/hold and experience the complete AR effect. This is of particular concern for the very young audiences of *Alex*, but also a consideration for the elderly. For similar technologies, such as VR systems, the impact of a wearable's weight and other elements that induce unwellness in participants is well documented (Chang et al., 2020). I have lived experience of this, with a visual impairment that makes participating in any encounter that requires a virtual headset extremely unpleasant, resulting in waves of vertigo and nausea that can last for hours after removing the device.

Though, technologists are yet to develop a method for those who are blind or severely visually impaired to fully participate in the kinds of augmentations described here, closed caption descriptions can operate in most modern theatre venues, which CARL encounters should attempt to also incorporate. There is also the comparably trifling but considerably frustrating reality of ensuring smart devices are adequately charged and powered, save switching off mid-experience and taking the participant completely out of the augmented world. For those with ways unique to them of operating within the world, who may not be able to manage the pre-charging and forward planning for such an experience, CARL alleviates many of these obstacles to participating in an AR encounter.

"It's alive... It's alive, it's moving ... IT'S ALIVE!": Realtime manipul/augment/ation

Crucial to *Alex* and its attempts to preserve the liveness of theatre to the greatest extent possible, and the resulting impact this has on the communal aspect of CARL, was the real-time manipulation of the animation by the physical theatre performer. Contrast this with another common practice within the theatre, whereby video and/or animation effects are pre-recorded and then simply played during the performance as filmic elements of the work, *Alex* required the live manipulation of the animated AR effects. The desire was to preserve as much of the reactionary magic as possible between the real and animated characters. Thus, enabling live adjustments by the actors to each other's performative offerings and to the audience reactions. This further enhances the irreplicable nature of live performance, which is one of its most unique and desirable elements, where each audience member brings their own experiences and perspectives to the performance (Heim, 2020, p. 30), enabling a nuanced and distinctive theatrical experience sensitive to and aligned with each audience and audience member for each and every performance.

Enabling real-time manipulation of the animation by a real-life actor means that both onstage and backstage performers can 'work-off' each other and facilitate the organic unfolding of the story each night. This allows for the nuance and subtlety of each performer's acting and reacting to evolve with each showing, adapting to each other's energy as well as to the audience's reactions and responses to the story unfolding before them. In addition to the motion capture camera system set up for the backstage performer, the actor was also provided with a live camera feed of the action onstage. This meant they could see their fellow cast members as well as their own animated performance, further facilitating the live action/interaction elements of the CARL experience.

Some may argue that the actor operating the animation backstage need not be in the same physical space as the rest of the action, given that they are provided with a video feed of what is happening onstage in real time. However, as ineffable as it may be, there is a shared energy and atmosphere that envelops a live performance space. Those familiar with an active theatre, a packed sports stadium or a field full of music festival concertgoers inherently understand the inexplicable way in which the entire space seems to 'breathe' with the production, every action and reaction infecting the energy and feeling of the cast, crew and audience. This does not translate through video feeds. As a theatre maker and regular audience member, I believe this phenomenon is more than worthy to maintain.

CARL requires an audience to share the same physical space and moment in time as each other and the actors, and crucially with the actor/performer manipulating the digitally augmented AR character(s). This ensures the collective, synchronous experience known and expected of a live theatrical event is maintained even with the digitally augmented character. While individual perceptions of augmented or virtual reality environments vary even when experienced synchronously, due to each individual's own interpretation of the event based on their distinctive lived experiences and unique perspectives as independent human beings (Woycicki, 2021), CARL maintains the communal empathy, collective catharsis and shared interactions central to dramatic storytelling through the theatrical artform.

Unlike virtual reality, for example, which immerses individuals in a separate digital world, CARL embeds virtual elements within the real environment, allowing audiences to encounter these elements without direct interaction/distraction with the technology that enabled the augmentation. CARL preserves the shared interactions and communal empathy central to Aristotelean dramatic storytelling. Unlike virtual reality, which immerses individuals in a separate digital world, CARL integrates virtual elements into the shared and very real environment. This approach allows audiences to encounter digital augmentations without direct technological interaction, embedding the digital alongside the tangible.

I like to move it, move it: MoCap

The MoCap controls used by the physical theatre performer in *Alex* were a bespoke design, fashioned from a reverse-engineered, commercially available gaming console motion capture system. The out-of-the-box hardware was retooled to work most accurately within the near-zero light conditions of the theatre's backstage. It was originally intended to track both broad movements of the body, as well as detailed intricacies of a performer's facial expressions. With this system, the performer was able to wear their usual clothing, appropriate for the physicality and free movement required, without the need for a specialist MoCap suit with its requisite dots/trackers for the camera to recognise their body and its motion. This system provided perhaps the greatest potential in the desire to incorporate the holographic into a live theatre context, but as will be unpacked, it became one of the most disappointing components of the CARL method in this example.

The movement captured by the system, provided by the performer backstage, was relayed to a projected animation in real-time. Thrown to the onstage gauze, which was hidden within the performance space to form an invisible element of the set design. The animated character was intended to be an immediate expression/replication of the performer controlling it. The analogy would be a puppet and puppeteer, only in this case, the puppet was a holographic-effect projection, and the puppeteer was the dancer/performer, backstage. The strings, as it were, not literally pulled by the performer to manipulate the animated character, but rather represented by the data cables connecting the motion capture cameras to the lighting and effects desk and ultimately the rigged projector, transferring the motion provided by the performer, and captured by the camera, before being released through the projector as the holo-effect animation (Figure 3.1).

He has a point: The rationale for using CARL in live performance

The question arises: why use AR technology when, conceivably, a cast of exclusively 'real' actors could suffice? Live theatre has survived as long as it has by creating characters with the assistance of make-up, costume, puppetry, projection, and mask acting. Arguably, established theatrical devices to imply and represent other-worldly characters are preferable, given the existing skill set of performers to bring them to life, the familiarity with the practical and technical conventions of a theatre to support their performance, and the established audience codes that viewers are willing to accept and buy-in to their presentation onstage.

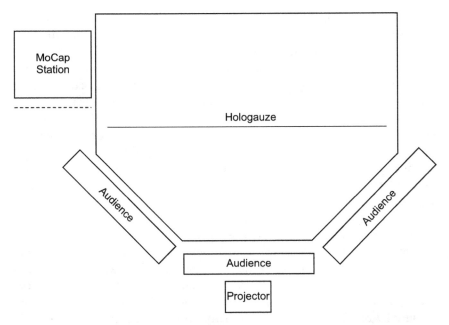

FIGURE 3.1 Stage diagram showing Hologauze and MoCap Station placement.

Fundamentally, the vision for the character of Alex included abilities that were beyond the very real physical constraints of the actor and a world governed by physics. Alex was required to perform such feats as floating, flying, and other characters transforming from humanoids into a whirlwind of pickled cucumbers. Yes, these effects could have been achieved through clever costuming, puppets or props, fly and pulley systems, projection mapping and other video wizardry, but if there was access to AR technology that could also enable these effects, why not use it? If there is no question about incorporating standard theatrical effects, then there is an argument that the same level of acceptance should also be applied to the implementation of new or emerging theatrical tools.

However, translating these ideas into believable digital effects was consistently challenging. The technical demands of AR required extensive rehearsal and practical adjustments. This process was further complicated by venue constraints and unfamiliarity with the technology, leading to last-minute reconfigurations and increased production costs. It seemed that many of the opportunities for this technology to overcome some of the limitations of the physical world, which are provided as a rationale for using the technology in the first place, were not yet realisable to the level hoped.

In practice, real-time manipulated digital characters may require an actor to learn, or at least upskill, in the techniques required to perform for the bespoke motion capture system. Lighting designers and technicians must shift their understandings of traditional theatre illumination, adjusting angles, lamp type and placement to enhance the efficacy of the holographic gauze and avoid interfering with the effect. Sound designers must recalibrate their usual aural scheme to overcome the impact of the gauze, which provides an invisible barrier between the performer and audience, sometimes requiring additional micing so that onstage voices are not redirected/bounced off the gauze to the rear or ceiling of the auditorium. Onstage actors must learn to work with the gauze and the projection, which is also invisible to their eye, and provide the audience with the illusion that they have full movement across the stage, when they are significantly inhibited by a giant, invisible wall, from which they cannot break free.

But, perhaps, most crucially, audiences must accept and, in some ways, agree to re-learn their relationship with the onstage world – reassess their willingness to suspend disbelief. Animations on TV or in a holo-zoo are one thing, but to witness a clearly cartoon-character, like Alex, onstage and alongside real-life actors initiates a different, some might say new, agreement between the audience and onstage action. Theatre audiences are discerning by reflex. The simple act of sitting in an auditorium and willingly giving your time and imagination to the performance sparks an undeniable expectation amongst audiences, demanding that the performance will provide them with an equal quid-pro-quo to the personal investment they have made in it.

To this end, a CARL-enabled production must meet perhaps an even higher effects standard than a traditional piece of theatre. The technology must work seamlessly, and the augmentation must truly align with the aims of the narrative and support the dramatic action. This is the same for any use of technology within live performance, whether that be the ancient scene-changing devices introduced by the Greeks or late 20th-century AV projections; the technology must be integral and not superficial, or audiences may reject it.

The road to an AR hellscape is paved with good intentions: The problems encountered

Fundamentally, *Alex* was a great success, with positive audience feedback for the work overall and findings that proved the use of the AR technology in live performance can work in a commercial context and is desirable to audiences. However, while every creative project is unique, one universal experience for theatre makers may be the hiccups in the production process that are commonplace. Indeed, I may even be so bold as to suggest that almost every live theatrical performance that has ever been produced in the world's entire history would have experienced some kind of problem, ranging in severity anywhere along the scale of "the audience won't even notice" to "this is a complete disaster – cancel opening night." *Alex* was no exception, and while the show did go on, as it must, the particular circumstances that the work found itself in due to its AR requirements did, on one estimation, increase the risk to the production's success and inflame what may have otherwise been simpler challenges to overcome. While no single element or person can rightly be labelled as the root cause of the obstacles the production found in its path, there is a series of events that culminated in the season, at one point, being cancelled and ticket sales halted.

The issues *Alex* faced can be broadly allocated into one of three categories: the infrastructural, the technological and the economic. While none of these three are particular to an AR theatre work, each was somehow conflated by the demands of the AR elements and their centrality to the overall dramaturgical design and creative form. By discussing these things here, the intention is not to dwell nor to deter others from working with this kind of technology by demonstrating any particular struggles it may bring to a creative project. The desire is to detail some of the more prominent issues this project faced in a spirit of collegiality and honesty, so that others who wish to, might learn from these struggles or, perhaps even more joyously, empathise with their own experiences of theatre making and share in the catharsis – or perhaps even schadenfreude – that comes from witnessing the familiar downfalls of contemporaries in the field. The chapter will now proceed to detail these categories of issues in turn, demonstrating not only how each contributed to the temporary cancellation of the project before opening night but also using these examples to arrive at possible contingencies other similar endeavours may wish to consider before embarking on their own AR theatre project.

"Oh, the humanity," – the infrastructural (physical and organisational) issues that were almost Alex's own Hindenburg

The effects used in a CARL piece of theatre such as *Alex*, require specific equipment. As detailed above, this equipment includes a specialist and sizeable piece of holographic gauze, a high-powered projector, a desk equipped with capacity to operate the projector, a bespoke motion capture system set up backstage, and a computer/hardware that can receive the feed from the MoCap system, render it through animation software to manipulate the animated character, before sending this digital signal to the desk where it is transposed into an image via the projector and gauze. A standard theatre rig generally includes a projector, some kind of drop that can act as a scrim or screen and a lighting desk connected to a computer running standard operating software such as QLab, controlling AV, Snd and LX cues. While analogous, the standard theatre equipment – projector, scrim, and computer-controlled operating board – are not the same as the high-powered projector, Hologauze and MoCap system required for *Alex*. Not only is the equipment not the same, but the skills and knowledge to bump-in, focus, plot, and operate can require specialists, particularly where the animation and real-time relay are concerned.

In the months leading up to *Alex*, there were several site visits, emails, phone calls and in-person discussions with venue technicians and technical managers. During this period, several potential problems and solutions were negotiated, and by and large it was agreed that the project would bring with it mostly its own equipment and specialist staff, effectively using the venue to house the production but fitted out and run by the team behind *Alex*. These arrangements appeared in line with the venue hire agreement, understanding it is not outside common industry practice for productions to truck in their own equipment and technicians, particularly when specific skillsets and hardware are required. However, several days before the production was set to bump-in, the venue took a different direction and decided to rely on in-house equipment and labour to set up the production.

The project would now only be permitted to use the venue's equipment and staff. Our technologists, technicians, animators, designers, and production and stage managers would not be permitted to enter the venue for bump-in. Our team would only be allowed to work with the equipment when a negotiated rehearsal time in the venue began. This rehearsal period was considerably shorter than originally planned. *Alex*'s specialist theatre equipment was also not allowed to be used in the space due to an interpretation of legal liability: that if we used our own staff and equipment and something went wrong, then the venue would be responsible. A legitimate concern for any venue, given the often-limited resources available to deal with any potentially harmful outcomes. Though, attempts to reconcile this concern with the venue hire agreement, particularly related to external equipment and the formal passing of liability, were not resolved. Uncertainty around the feasibility of the show to go ahead under these conditions impacted the marketing strategy and public messaging, temporarily shutting down the project and affecting ticket sales and audience numbers.

This little diversion into the gritty reality of organisational intervention into the creative process demonstrates the importance of adjusting how some of the more pragmatic and practical elements of making theatre may be approached when applying AR technologies to achieve effects like CARL in a traditional, commercial theatre space. To sincerely tour a work like *Alex*, which began in the technologically resourced environment of a University of Technology, into an established theatre venue would be made simpler with upgrades to existing venue infrastructure. Supplementing existing electrical and digital multiplex (DMX) cabling, for example, with high-speed ethernet connections and ensuring bio box computer systems have been installed and can run animation tools such as Unreal Engine, would be an ideal scenario. If this had been the case, the show could have been more easily ported into the venue. As it was, after requesting a list of the show's technical and other requirements from the *Alex* team, it was discovered the venue did not stock the equipment and digital infrastructure needed to make the show a reality. The project then lent its equipment, which was taken to the venue and left at the entrance to the backstage loading dock, for internal venue contractors to install.

After entering the venue, it was discovered that several technical elements were either missing or incorrectly installed for use alongside AR effects. While the specialised equipment needed to capture, digitise, and display the digital augmentations was one consideration, the impact these technologies have on established elements of theatrical design also comes into play. The *Alex* lighting designer had incorporated elements to enhance the world of the play, without interfering with the operation of the Hologauze and alleviating any risk that lamps would wash-out the projected effects. This included fundamental considerations about where to place and how to focus the lamps, specifically on a stage fitted with Hologauze. In practice, the lamps had been hung for a stage that might have been set with a scrim, or backdrop, requiring re-adjustment and re-focusing before rehearsals could begin. The stage masking was also inadequate for the light control required for projected Hologauze effects. The gauze itself hung to incorrect measurements, resulting in damage and eventually found to have a tear. Sound equipment, too, remained in a standard position, with speakers located behind the Hologauze, obstructing the soundwave trajectory and interfering with audibility.

The incongruousness between certain, established ways of using traditional theatre effects and the requirements of some new technologies highlights another opportunity for the cultivation of the theatrical form, particularly how we train and develop our skilled technicians. As the use of effects, such as AR, becomes more feasible in a live performance context, institutions – such as the University of Technology that seeded *Alex* – must continue to build the skills and knowledge required for their function into their training regimes. Similarly, the industry would do well to provide professional development opportunities not only to self-described artists, but also to interested technical crews to investigate, experiment with and develop new knowledge about these technologies and how they are practically applied.

One of the most impactful outcomes of these infrastructural speedbumps was a significant decrease in the amount of time afforded to the cast and creative team to prepare and work with the technology in the space.

This was further exacerbated by issues with the technology itself, which will be detailed in the following section. All these practical and organisational elements had to be dealt with before the actors and crew could run the show and it could be properly rehearsed in the space. As any producer knows, issues of infrastructure take a considerable amount of temporal resources, in this case, ultimately reducing the practice and rehearsal time by almost two days. The actors and technicians were exceptional in their acceptance of this and proved how resilient, determined and adaptable artists can be. Though, as a director, I still lament the limited capacity I was able to give them to do their best work, robbing them of the time and focus they otherwise would have had to showcase their skills in this experiment. Some of the problems, including the stage masking and gauze placement, were never properly fixed and had to simply be patched and solved to whatever extent possible, resulting in an overall appearance for the production that, as a director with my name on the thing, I considered unacceptable.

Updating our theatre and live performance spaces to ensure that next-generation technologies can function seamlessly will be critical to maintaining a relevant and current live performance industry that can capitalise on AR and other emerging technologies. This would also contribute to the tourability of such works, increasing potential audiences for show producers and providing exposure to the latest innovations in creativity for diverse groups of theatregoers. The ability to articulate technological requirements clearly and be afforded plenty of time for the practical processes that make them work, such as bumping-in and rehearsing, will improve any production outcome. Perhaps, even, flexibility and acknowledgement of the unpredictability of the creative process by makers and venues alike, particularly when negotiating projects that use new and novel techniques requiring an alteration to traditional theatre-making approaches, could be taken into consideration as part of the commercial contracting process. Furthermore, developing industry knowledge and skills with and about new technologies is crucial for their practical application. All parties, including administrators, holding even a cursory understanding of the technology and how it works, and how it might interact with existing theatre infrastructure, proves vital to the success of these kinds of projects.

"Don't be too proud of this technological terror you've constructed." – The technological issues that almost destroyed Alex's *world*

Throughout the three-week period before relocating to the venue, the show had been rehearsing full-time in a blackbox studio in a separate location from where the performance season would be held. The studio had been fitted with a faux-holographic screen, a sharkstooth gauze and a smaller projector that could be used in lieu of the full-scale Hologauze and the powerful projector it required. A rehearsal 'MoCap' system was also in place, which was simply a video camera connected to the projector so that the performers could experience the projected character effect. This rehearsal version of the system did not include the animation; it was the actual actor that was filmed and displayed on the sharkstooth scrim. Helpfully, the rehearsal space was close in proximity to a full-scale virtual production studio, which is also fitted with a high-end motion capture system, housed by QUT, which we were able to access for specific sessions during this preliminary rehearsal period. Having access to this studio gave the performers the opportunity to practice with an actual MoCap system, in anticipation of the eventual performance at the premiere season venue. This also demonstrates the connections between film-technologies, such as virtual production, and live performance, exemplifying how the theatre, in this case, can borrow from other digitised artforms to explore the potential for new ways of creative expression.

During the rehearsal process in the virtual production studio, the animator on the project was able to access and manipulate the animations through virtual production software in real time as the performer was controlling the digital characters through the motion capture system. This meant that any adjustments related to motion retargeting, real-time rendering and so on could be done in the moment, generating a most responsive representation of the Alex character. The motion capture system accessed at QUT also allowed for intricate details of the performer's facial expression to be captured and transferred to the face of the animated character. These elements were critical to the brief provided to the technologists who were contracted to supply the motion capture system and Alex animation for the production. The ability to access and tinker with root data for the animation and to capture the most intricate of facial movements was identified early in the process as key to ensuring a high-quality, theatrically refined outcome for the AR elements of the production.

However, when the final version of the Alex character arrived and the motion capture system was installed backstage in the performance venue, issues quickly arose. The data provided for the animation was supplied as part of a closed system. It seems this happened in the process of copying the files to make them portable to the computer system in the performance venue. The files were, effectively, locked and could not be altered or changed neither in preparation for the performance, nor in real time during the performance. The original intention was that the files would be completely open to alteration by the production team, even during the performance season.

This led to all kinds of issues when attempting to calibrate the system in the performance venue. The animation constantly appeared too far above or below its intended position onstage, with its anchor completely off-kilter. This created issues with the audience's perspective and ultimately threatened to undermine the entire believability of the character. This could destroy any audience buy-in to the empathetic relationship that is required to successfully create drama: if an audience is too busy laughing at how a character looks, especially when it is not meant to be funny, they are never going to invest in its place in the story. A version of the data that could be altered by the Alex animator was later sourced; however, as became the hallmark of this project, it was at the eleventh hour and allowed only for emergency fixes and renderings to have the animation at a passable level for public presentation. The result was far from the intended, and not to the same level of finesse that we had been able to achieve during rehearsals within the virtual production studio.

The other most prominent issue we faced with the technology presented itself in the tailor-made motion capture system provided for the production. The brief was to develop a smaller-scale and portable version of a larger MoCap system. With far fewer resources and the requirement to be portable, it was never expected that the production version of this setup would deliver the exact same results as the equipment we had been using as part of the pre-rehearsal process in the virtual production studio. However, the ability to track and replicate facial expression, even broadly, was a key component. Upon installation, it was soon discovered that the system had a limited ability to capture even movements of the arms and legs that occurred too speedily, let alone detect the nuances of the actor's face. The equipment fell short of expectations and required a complete reshaping of the performer's movements for the entire show, which the choreographer and performers miraculously achieved in a single afternoon.

It is no secret that the use of any technology, particularly something new and not used in the show previously, should be made available and tested well in advance of a performance opening week. Indeed, to proceed in any other way may seem like a rooky mistake and many may be levelling that very accusation at me for progressing *Alex* in the way it was. This is something the entire creative team was aware of and had been agitating for throughout the process. In the dizzying reality of it all, though, everything occurred exactly as it did and arrived exactly as it was and only when it could, for a myriad of reasons outside of anyone one person's control. At this point and when confronted with such a situation, there is not much that any theatre maker can do except to remind themselves of that quote from the film *Shakespeare in Love* (Madden, 1998, 1:19):

Philip Henslowe: Mr. Fennyman, allow me to explain about the theatre business. The natural condition is one of insurmountable obstacles on the road to imminent disaster.
Hugh Fennyman: So what do we do?
Philip Henslowe: Nothing. Strangely enough, it all turns out well.
Hugh Fennyman: How?
Philip Henslowe: I don't know. It's a mystery.

"The two cardinal rules of producing ... Never put your own money in the show ... and ... never put your own money in the show!" – The financial considerations that impacted AR in Alex

Live, commercial theatre is expensive. *Alex* was only possible with funding support from local and state government, a philanthropic trust, a research centre dedicated to exploring new ways to design creative experiences, and in-kind support from collaborators. For all this support, the project team were extremely grateful and acknowledge that, in no small way, this is what enabled the overall success of the production. In-kind access to rehearsal space and technologies, provided by QUT, was also crucial to the eventual realisation of the work. Significantly, the time and research capacity provided by experts in animation, dramaturgy, choreography and digital scenography from QUT also made the project possible and ensured positive outcomes. As someone who has run independent theatre companies in the past, I am inclined to say that working with this kind of technology on this scale would not be possible without significant government and third-party funding, and the in-kind contributions of time and expertise provided by the project team and enabled/funded by a university. In this respect, the resources required to deliver such a project appear inhibitive, somewhat limiting the possible application and delivery of this kind of CARL experience in other circumstances.

What makes this example, and the AR experiences it represents, more costly, is the requirement to not only include traditional theatre roles – actors, designers, technicians, and operators – but also recruit specialist animators, immersive experience technologists and programmers/coders. In this case, the production costs appeared to double with the inclusion of the specialist roles and contractors. This was further exacerbated by the infrastructural and technological hiccups described above, particularly the disruptions to ticket sales that had a material impact on production income. Without the luxury of external funding, the hit to box office takings would have sunk the entire project. In the end, we were able to offer free and heavily discounted tickets to ensure healthy audiences. This is not a luxury often afforded to theatre makers, and the cost of creating CARL experiences like this is currently, therefore, a serious consideration when embarking on such a project.

Only by large institutions, such as universities, State theatre companies and government departments, investing in and experimenting with these technologies now, will we find sustainable ways to embed them into our creative practices. If institutions undertake to continue developing and experimenting with these and other technologies, we will begin to understand how they are best applied and provide opportunities to build the skills and knowledge of the industry to adapt them into their practices. This may seem counter to the idea that AR effects are the next natural evolution in theatre and live stage effects; however, there is always a period of cost-prohibitive when new technologies emerge. It is incumbent on larger institutions to invest during this period, so that the next generation of makers and audiences are prepared, and to ensure that the sector does not miss the opportunity altogether, finding itself in a situation where only the super-profits of K-pop are able to access the latest innovations, having stitched-up the market to ensure inaccessibility and maintain a monopoly on the invention.

99 Problems…, A summary to this section and discussion on AI enhanced AR

In the opening anecdote of this chapter, detailing *Star Trek*'s Holodeck as the inspiration behind this experimentation, I make a deliberate distinction between what I term traditional theatre experience, and that which would be considered an immersive theatre experience, which has its own body of theory and practice (Machon, 2013). While some may aim to replicate a level of interactivity in AR, my objective diverges. I believe that transforming audience members into active participants veers towards gamification, blurring the lines between theatrical play and gameplay, narrative and ludonarrative (Howe, 2017). My work focuses on enhancing traditional theatrical experiences through character and scenographic augmentations, maintaining the integrity of the shared audience experience and the place of the audience as observer, though not entirely passive but active in their intellectual and imaginative interaction with the play. This is where Rodenberry and I depart on our envisioned future for AR and its place as entertainment and artform: while Starfleet officers may play on the Holodeck, it was the actors of *Alex* who played onstage for their audience. This decision is not a judgement about interactive theatre nor theatre that is not interactive; it is simply a preference as a theatre maker that I have, and that I also share as an audience member. I much prefer to have a story unfold onstage before me than to be asked to physically 'act' in that story myself.

An obvious benefit to the enhancement of live performance using CARL enabling technologies can be identified in the unique capabilities of digital characters, brought to life by the kind of technological application evidenced in *Alex*. The digital character in Alex was able to transcend physical limitations that a human performer would be inhibited by, enabling the backstage-hologram operator to also transcend the limits of their body and the physical world, safely. Traditional theatrical effects, such as fly systems and pyrotechnics, pose clear safety risks and require complex and specialised training and equipment. While there may be additional training required of performers when using MoCap-associated systems, in general AR technology offers a safer, more accessible alternative. Particularly, as it is argued will happen, the technology continues to evolve and become more agile, user-friendly and intuitive, and less costly, eventually democratising advanced theatrical effects to be used by a greater variety of theatre makers.

The converse argument may be that, rather than soliciting a transcendence from the physical limitations of the human performer, incorporating this kind of augmentation into live performance inhibits the performer's creativity and the clever artistry of the live artist. Without the technology, performers and their directors and choreographers are required to invent ways to imply the transcendence of the physical. Rather than having the character fly up and across the stage as an animation, creativity must be harnessed to devise a sequence of movements and theatrical inferences that imply to the audience the action of flight. This is perhaps the most poetic element of live theatre and an example of its most fundamental elements as an artform. It would be wise to consider, whether replacing this kind of creative imagination with a digital character's ability to 'actually' fly up into the air and across the stage, devalues the poetic credibility of live theatrical performance, and encourages performance makers to abandon those elements of the artform that render its creativity most legitimate.

To fully consider this argument, we must look to the history of theatre and assess how it has dealt with the advancement of other technologies. From this perspective, it is arguable to see that the inclusion of AR technology in live performance is more likely to complement the evolution of live theatre, developing as an additional tool available to the theatre maker to assist them to realise their creative vision(s). The application of advancements in understandings of visual perspective did not diminish the creativity of the theatrical scene maker, indeed, it arguably enabled them a greater depth – pun intended – of creative expression. Similarly, the evolution of the proscenium to mask fly and pulley systems did not dampen the audience buy-in when literally flying actors across the stage, just as audiences did not reject the use of stage lighting to create fake daylight. The inclusion of projected images and immersive soundscapes in live theatre has undeniably enhanced the overall potential of the theatrical experience when embraced by theatre makers as an inextricable tool to support their deepest desires for dramaturgical world-making. Based on these examples, it is logical to argue that the inclusion of AR technology in live performance will enhance the theatrical encounter and outcome rather than diminish the human creativity that is inherent in the artform.

Upon reflection with key contributors in the project – writer/director, animator, choreographer, dramaturg, and digital scenographer/audience researcher – and their experiences creating CARL in a traditional theatre setting, it was also envisioned how developing AI systems might enhance similar collaborations in the future. AI-driven platforms, which process large data sets to recognise patterns and adapt processes traditionally performed by humans (EVOLVAI, 2025), and AI-generated content, which creates images, words, and animations (Zhang et al., 2024), were identified as technologies most likely to enhance the CARL experience for live theatre. It was decided that AI presents significant potential to streamline and improve the integration of AR. For instance, imagine AI-generated motion capture responding to commands from a CARL theatre designer, allowing for real-time adjustments of computer animation effects during rehearsals. The designer prompts the system to fly a character in a spiral at the immediate request of the director, or its MoCap operating performer. The creatives are able to view the offer as soon as it is suggested and make adjustments on the floor as required. This iterative process mirrors traditional scene rehearsals, integrating AR as a natural extension of the dramatic composition. However, it was also discussed that the concept of 'Responsible Innovation' is crucial (Piskopani et al., 2023). While AI can improve creative workflows and safety, it is decidedly essential to preserve the role of human specialists in the creative process.

If the technology is harnessed effectively, then the opportunities it affords to the evolution of live performance are considerable. Institutions must continue to invest in the technology at this experimental stage to find ways of enhancing its accessibility and affordability, and encourage emerging makers to push the boundaries, so as the technology becomes increasingly portable and affordable, the opportunities for smaller theatres and independent artists to employ it in their own works will inherently grow. In the not-too-distant future, it is likely we will see AR applied in all kinds of creative ways onstage that we have not yet even conceived. The vision is of a future CARL play efficiently achieving significant effects that would currently require, at least based on this example, considerable resources and human expertise, rendered increasingly possible as AR tools become more accessible and economical, aided by accompanying developments in AI.

Living next door to *Alex*: Background to the project, AR theatre as healthcare intervention

The 2023 La Boite production of *Alex* was not the first iteration of the play. It was the commercial realisation of an earlier production, originally an applied theatre performance fusing ethnodrama and ethnotheatre practices (Saldaña, 2011) with augmented reality technology to develop an arts-based intervention in a healthcare context. This included young people with eating disorders as participants, who shared their stories and lived experiences to contribute to the development of the ethnodramatic script that became the AR-infused ethnotheatrical performance. As an intervention in a healthcare context, the augmented reality effect – the hologram character – existed as a kind of avatar for the participants, expressing and demonstrating in animated form a dramatised representation of their lived experiences with and within their bodies. The aim was to provide a way for them to demonstrate, through the manipulation and projection of an animated character, how certain situations, triggers and everyday interactions, made them feel about their bodies. Or, perhaps more accurately, provide them with a visual aid that could demonstrate externally to others how they perceived their own bodies in their own minds.

In this way, the holographic effect/character was able to express and demonstrate not only to themselves but also to other audience members, in a visual sense, the internalisation of negative thought patterns that often drove their condition. Their families, healthcare workers and other researchers were provided an insight into how they felt and perceived their bodies, in a way that would not otherwise have been possible simply by describing or attempting to draw/sketch a representation of the internal image they held of themselves. The projected animation also acted as a literal, though still digital, representation of the destructive voice ever-present in their minds, able to be manipulated and rendered by them to provide an accurate, visual example of their internal negative thoughts through the animated character. It also provided the participants the opportunity to see for themselves how their internalised voice and its projected self-image appeared in the physical world, expressed through the humanoid, holographic projection.

The version of *Alex* that forms the substantive component of this chapter, while not produced with the main aim of acting as a healthcare intervention, retained its core themes of mental and physical health. While these themes featured in the so-called moral of the story, and were subsequently employed to underscore the dramatic action, they were not the core of the project as practice-led research. Rather, the commercial realisation of the work at La Boite, was an experiment with two main research aims: to test the validity of using the AR technology in a commercial theatre context; and to gather preliminary data on mainstream audience reactions to incorporating this type of AR technology alongside traditional theatre practices. Ultimately, the creators wanted to know whether the technology was portable from a university research space into a traditional commercial theatre space, and once transported, whether audiences would accept and/or desire this technology as part of their usual theatrical experience. From these two separate but related applications, the application of AR technology in theatre is rendered useful in both an arts-clinical context, as well as for commercial theatre.

Conclusion: But hopefully not the end for Alex

The project *Alex* exemplifies one approach to integrating AR in theatre, an example of a CARL play. The goal was to preserve the traditional audience experience as much as possible, while leveraging AR technology to enhance onstage narratives and support actors to achieve otherwise impossible physicality of character. It was hypothesised that these advancements could benefit both performers and audiences, without requiring direct audience interaction with the technology. Instead, the AR character, Alex, was designed to interact with live performers, creating a blending of digital and physical onstage. Despite the problems encountered, the experience was overall a success and presented to a keen general, public audience, demonstrating that there is potential for this technology to be utilised within a commercial theatre context, outside of the technology-arts-research studio. However, there are elements to consider when embedding this kind of effect into live theatre, not least of which are the additional costs currently associated with producing the augmentations. The further considerations around infrastructure and resourcing, as well as access to the technology and an appropriate amount of time to test it, are also important.

In terms of audience acceptance and/or desire to experience this type of AR effect as part of their theatregoing encounters, overall, the feedback was promising. Audiences surveyed as part of this, and the earlier healthcare intervention versions of *Alex* clearly expressed a positive outlook for the potential of this kind of experience in a live theatre context. Audiences were open and willing to see more works using CARL effects and recorded an overwhelmingly positive response when questioned whether or not it enhanced their theatrical experience.

Survey respondents were, however, quick to identify any shortcomings of the technology used, picking up on even the slightest glitches in the animation. Attendees pointing out the deficiencies already known in terms of the sometimes-imperfect anchoring of the holographic effect within the staged scene. The issues with the sound were also noted by audiences, showing that even the most interesting of holographic effects are not enough to distract them from their overall expectations of a theatrical experience. In a formal data-gathering process of reflective discussion with the creative team, it was also decided that the infrastructural and technological issues experienced had an overall undesirable impact on the aesthetic outcomes of the work; however, the dramatic strength of the narrative and quality of the performances functioned to maintain the overall artistic integrity of the production.

Integrating AR technology in live performance offers exciting possibilities for enhancing traditional theatre. By balancing innovation with the preservation of the shared audience experience, richer, more dynamic performances may be created. The project *Alex* demonstrates both the potential and challenges of this integration, highlighting some of the possibilities of pursuing innovation in the evolving landscape of theatre and technology.

References

Auslander, P. (2022). *Liveness: Performance in a Mediatized Culture*. Taylor & Francis Group. https://ebookcentral.proquest.com/lib/qut/detail.action?docID=7127484

Australia's Oldest Boldest Theatre. (2024). La Boite. Retrieved 20 September, 2024 from https://laboite.com.au/about

Bourdot, P., Raya, M. A., Figueroa, P., Interrante, V., Kuhlen, T., & Reiners, D. (2021). Preface. *Virtual Reality and Mixed Reality 18th EuroXR International Conference*, Milan, Italy.

Brilli, S., Gemini, L., & Giuliani, F. (2023). Theatre without theatres: Investigating access barriers to mediatized theatre and digital liveness during the covid-19 pandemic. *Poetics*, *97*, 101750. https://doi.org/10.1016/j.poetic.2022.101750

Chang, E., Kim, H. T., & Yoo, B. (2020). Virtual reality sickness: A review of causes and measurements. *International Journal of Human–Computer Interaction*, *36*(17), 1658–1682. https://doi.org/10.1080/10447318.2020.1778351

Chang, W., & Shin, H. D. (2019). Virtual experience in the performing arts: K-live hologram music concerts. *Popular Entertainment Studies*, *10*(1–2), 34–50.

EOLVAI (2025, May 1). *What is AI-driven?* https://evolv.ai/glossary/ai-driven

Heim, C. (2020). *Actors and Audiences: Conversations in the Electric Air*. Taylor & Francis Group. https://ebookcentral.proquest.com/lib/qut/detail.action?docID=6130890

Howe, L. A. (2017). Ludonarrative dissonance and dominant narratives. *Journal of the Philosophy of Sport*, *44*(1), 44–54. https://doi.org/10.1080/00948705.2016.1275972

Machon, J. (2013). *Immersive Theatres: Intimacy and Immediacy in Contemporary Performance*. Red Globe Press. https://search.ebscohost.com/login.aspx?direct=true&AuthType=sso&db=nlebk&AN=1522736&site=ehost-live&scope=site&custid=qut

Madden, J. (1998). *Shakespeare in Love* [Film]. Miramax.

Mercer, P. (2023, 20 October). Why a 'hologram revolution' could be on the way. *BBC News*. https://www.bbc.com/news/business-67080941

Meyer-Dinkgräfe, D. (2015). Liveness: Phelan, auslander, and after. *Journal of Dramatic Theory and Criticism*, *29*(2), 69–79. https://doi.org/10.1353/dtc.2015.0011

Phelan, P. (1993). *Unmarked: The Politics of Performance*. Taylor & Francis Group. https://ebookcentral.proquest.com/lib/qut/detail.action?docID=179272

Pike, S. (2019). "Make it so": Communal augmented reality and the future of theatre and performance. *Fusion Journal* (15), 108–118. doi:10.3316/informit.975162255148822

Piskopani, A. M., Chamberlain, A., & Ten Holter, C. (2023). Responsible AI and the Arts: The Ethical and Legal Implications of AI in the Arts and Creative Industries. *First International Symposium on Trustworthy Autonomous Systems, Tas 2023*, 1–5. https://doi.org/10.1145/3597512.3597528

Rosvally, D., & Sherman, D. (2023). *Early Modern Liveness: Mediating Presence in Text, Stage and Screen*. Bloomsbury Publishing Plc. https://ebookcentral.proquest.com/lib/qut/detail.action?docID=7131875

Saldaña, J. (2011). *Ethnotheatre: Research from Page to Stage*. Taylor & Francis Group. https://ebookcentral.proquest.com/lib/qut/detail.action?docID=795261

Speicher, M., Hall, B. D., & Nebeling, M. (2019). *What is Mixed Reality? Proceedings of the 2019 CHI Conference on Human Factors in Computing Systems*, Glasgow, Scotland UK. https://doi.org/10.1145/3290605.3300767

Woycicki, P. (2021). Interoceptive dramaturgies of 'surrogate-selves' in performative VR experiences. *Performance Research*, 26(3), 17–25. https://doi.org/10.1080/13528165.2021.1977492

Zhang, J. J., Wang, Y. W., Ruan, Q., & Yang, Y. (2024). Digital tourism interpretation content quality: A comparison between AI-generated content and professional-generated content. *Tourism Management Perspectives*, *53*, 101279. https://doi.org/10.1016/j.tmp.2024.101279

4

CASE STUDY 2: IMMERSIVE THEATRE IN EUROPE

CREW: VR innovators from Belgium (what we might learn from more established tech.)

In the previous chapter, the case study deliberately seeks to avoid producing an immersive theatre experience, endeavouring to use evolving AR technologies to enhance the traditional, live theatre form and create a CARL play. However, there is no denying that immersivity and the use of AR and VR technologies are closely aligned. For many live performance makers, immersion is the goal and AR and/or VR the vehicles through which to achieve this end. In June, 2024, I sat down in person with Eric Joris, founder of the immersive performance company: CREW. At their studio headquarters in Sint-Jans-Molenbeek, just to the West of the Brussels city centre, Joris shared with me some of the lessons he has accumulated over more than 30 years of creating technology-infused, immersive, theatrical experiences.

In an hour-long discussion, we also reflected on the history of the company, Joris's background in arts and technology, the kinds of technology CREW have used in their works, and posited potential futures for technology within the theatrical arts. This chapter is a reflection on that discussion, traversing between comments, notions and ideas directly from Joris and my own thoughts and considerations inspired by this conversation. Attribution is given to points provided directly by CREW's founder, otherwise, the words can be taken as general considerations inspired by the interview, gathered from notes made during and after, upon listening to a recording of the session.

CREW is described as "an international team of researchers, performers, technologists, dramaturgs, musicians, programmers, writers and designers" and "an arts company crossing the boundaries of arts, science and technology" (*About CREW*, 2024). Established in 1990, the company has spearheaded the incorporation of virtual technologies into live theatrical

DOI: 10.4324/9781003521907-4

experiences, their works described as "...hybrid; the technological live art of CREW troubles installed categories of theatricality, leading to immersive embodied environments that challenge common notions of (tele)presence, spectatorship and (interactive) narration" (Vanhoutte & Wynants, 2011, p. 277).

The company is currently driven by Joris and his contemporary, Isjtar Vandebroeck. The prominent technology deployed by CREW is VR. To focus on a company that uses VR technology in a monograph that purports to also consider AR and AI technologies can be considered informative. CREW defines themselves as makers of immersive experiences and are established as one of the world's most practiced and qualified companies in doing so. With this in mind, the inference is that much can be learnt from their experiences with immersive technologies that can likely be applied, or at least considered, in the broader theatre and technology context, whether that be VR, AR, AI or any other example of new/emerging technology.

While not the aim of every tech-enabled/enhanced theatre work, there is no denying that the use of technology in live dramatic performances has developed a connection with immersivity in many examples, and many proponents of the use of this kind of technology in theatre are also interested in creating immersive experiences. The helpfulness of investigating CREW and their works is chiefly found, therefore, in their expertise in developing and delivering immersive environments. Their craft and skill in experimenting with technology and applying it in a theatrical context is also informative for any other makers interested in adopting similar practices. Conversely and in addition to this, there are some inferences that could be drawn from CREW's decades of experience with VR that can be used to delineate between it and AR. These differences are helpful to understand the potential opportunities and challenges that each present and how AR might be capitalised on to overcome some of the possible limitations identified with VR technology and its application as a theatrical experience.

CREW, technology, and immersive theatre

At the outset, it is useful to briefly consider immersive theatre more generally, given it is the theatrical form CREW is known for and is also being proposed as the factor to link investigating VR and technology in theatre more generally. Immersive theatre is an arguably diverse form, credited with roots in the participatory political art of the 1960s as well as being linked to drama and theatre in education (Sterling & McAvoy, 2017). Over time, immersive theatre has evolved to become seemingly ubiquitous with certain notions of technology in performance, particularly the use of what are considered interactive technologies, such as VR. With elements of gameplay and gaming narrative also featuring heavily in discussions of the form and its defining components, a further consideration when attempting to discuss it and its technology-enabled exemplars is the complexities of when virtual game worlds become examples of theatre and vice versa (see for example: Giannachi, 2004, pp. 89–94). Some suggest that the connections between theatre and gameplay are not unique to immersive theatre, however, and have existed throughout theatrical history (Bloom, 2018). While there are arguments to be made that particular VR experiences labelled as theatre are potentially more identifiable as gamified events, the position is taken that the works of CREW are theatrical experiences at their core, not least of which because Joris and the makers at CREW expressly and convincingly label them as such.

Taking into account the succinct and learned summary of the form pro-vided by Pamela Stirling and Mary McAvoy in their chapter, "Art, Pedagogy and Innovation: Tracing the roots of immersive theatre and practice" (2017), the key element of immersive theatre identified here is the evolution of the audience through their involvement with the experience. Providing a thorough assessment of the theories and writings of Gareth White (2012), Josephine Machon (2013), and Adam Alston (2013), Stirling and McAvoy offer the understanding that immersive theatre is audience **evolvement** through **involvement** and, specifically in relation to audience members and their active participation in the immersion, includes considerations of risk, agency and personal responsibility (2017, p. 96). Discussions of immersive theatre and its historical development have clearly been well articulated by others, including those above, so there is no need to replicate this here. Ultimately, the understanding that immersive theatre is differentiated from other forms of theatre by virtue of a specific kind of audience experience is adopted in this discourse.

Audience evolution is understood to be experiential, in that they are somehow changed through their involvement with/participation in the immersion rather than simply via witnessing the theatrical event, as the audi-ence of a non-immersive work may. However, much the same as a tradi-tional theatre experience, the audience change (evolution), it is assumed, could be intellectual, emotional, psychological or even physical, having experienced or 'felt' something because of their participation in the encoun-ter. On one estimation, then, the effect of the theatrical experience on an audience may not differ between immersive and non-immersive forms; it is the way – or method – in which that effect is achieved that differs. For tra-ditional theatre, it is generally through witnessing or watching the narrative unfold that audience change and impact is achieved. For immersive theatre, the act of involvement in the narrative is the means to achieve what has been termed the evolutionary change of the audience.

The transformation of theatrical experiences from passive spectatorship to active participation, exemplified in the immersive theatre form, has been a significant evolution in how audiences engage with theatrical narratives. This evolution has been notably influenced by immersive technologies in recent decades. Listening to a story in a conventional theatre setting is seen as a passive act. When the audience is placed within the story – whether through immersive theatre achieved with or without technologies such as AR/VR – the experience is fundamentally altered.

Immersive environments create a participatory dimension, where individuals move from observing the story to actively and often physically becoming part of it. This shift reshapes both the relationship between the audience and the narrative as well as the role of the artist in constructing this interaction. This participatory element, as a hallmark of immersive theatre, is also where the term 'participant' becomes relevant. For this kind of theatrical experience, it is often the case that the audience member is referred to as a participant. For the purposes of this chapter, then, it is pertinent to reinforce that the labels 'audience' and 'participant' are understood as interchangeable terms.

Motion, duality, and awareness: Some key elements for a successful immersive experience with technology

The element of motion, or an audience's ability to move through the performance space – and the performance world or narrative itself – is confirmed by Joris as critical in creating a successful immersive experience, particularly when using VR technology. The incorporation of movement could be seen as an established element of many immersive theatre experiences, whether featuring VR or otherwise, with Punchdrunk's renowned *Sleep no More* a prominent example of this. In this work, audience members are given the agency and encouraged to roam freely around the venue at their leisure. However, a broader consideration of the field may reveal that motion and/or audience movement is not necessarily a defining component of immersive theatre in general.

Back to Back theatre company's *Small Metal Objects* is performed in outdoor locations ranging from a Melbourne train station to a Wellington waterfront, a New York Ferry Terminal to a commercial lobby in Hong Kong, with audiences placed in a fixed seating position while the actors mingle through the everyday environment in front of them. The immersion is chiefly maintained through headsets, worn by the audience so that they may hear the actor's dialogue, as if they were the proverbial fly-on-the-wall, listening in to the private conversations represented by the dialogue taking place in a very public space. While immersed in the surroundings, the audience is stationary as the everyday world moves around them.

Extending the concept even further, in 2017, Jessica Wilson's *Passenger* rendered audience and performers static but moved the entire performance space: a roadworthy suburban bus that is driven around while the performance takes place inside, with the audience and actors immersed and encapsulated within the mobile event. While the bus moves through the streets, there is no agency afforded to the audience to dictate or decide how that motion unfolds, rendering them stationary despite their motoring performance venue. So, while movement and agency in when/where participants travel is critical to immersive experiences such as *Sleep no More*, it is not a requisite for immersivity for works like *Small Metal Objects* and *Passenger*. Joris stresses, however, audience motion, and agency to move, **is** a critical component of a successful immersive theatre experience using VR technology.

Traversing the complexity of movement and immersion further still are works such as Seth Kriebel's *The Unbuilt Room*, which takes place in an empty space, while Kriebel describes another world as part of the narrative journey. Audience members are encouraged to 'travel' through the imagined world, deciding which direction to turn, influencing the fantasy space and how they 'move' through it, in their mind's eye, as the experience unfolds. In this way, audiences are given the imagined perception of movement and motion through physical space, enhancing the interactivity of the work, but are, in reality, confined to a small room with the journey taking place entirely in their imaginations. It describes itself as a "piece of promenade theatre [audiences] undertake without lifting a finger" (Kriebel, n.d.).

Interactional motion: Imagination enabled by the virtual

The kind of experience offered by Kriebel, seems to exploit the theatre's inherent ability to invoke the human imagination through narrative. A complex process described by Michael Mangan as the 'transactional interactions' (2006) inherent in the imaginative reconstructions elicited by the theatre experience: that is, the images conjured in an audience's mind by the words and descriptions given by the actors onstage, or in this case, Kriebel's narration. Mangan also points out that this interaction between theatrical narrative and imagination is long-known, and was directly acknowledged by Shakespeare in the prologue to *Henry V*, where the chorus recites "On your imaginary forces work … For 'tis your thoughts that now must deck our Kings" and "think, when we talk of horses, that you see them" (Shakespeare et al., 1982, p. 93).

Arguably, the use of AR and VR technologies in live theatre is simply a new-age expression of Mangan's interactions and Shakespeare's choral prompts. The images conjured in the mind are now possible through animations/augmentations. For the story creator, the technology provides an additional level of control, ensuring that the images they intend are the ones the audience literally sees/experiences rather than a creation of each individual's imagination. A further point is whether the utilisation of these technologies to generate digital imagery and visual elements is another example of contemporary outsourcing for the human mind: audiences are no longer required to employ their imagination to colour the dramatic world; it is simply displayed for them.

However, there is another level of interaction with the Manganian reconstructions that are critical to a successful VR experience, confirmed in the discussion with Joris. The point here, whether the reconstruction is imagined or digitally presented, is interesting but adjacent to the consideration of how the audience interacts with that reconstruction. In the Shakesperean example, the interaction is purely cerebral, though it may inspire an emotional or even physical reaction. It is achieved through mostly verbal but also possibly visual cues by virtue of costume and props to be processed and imagined in the audience's minds via a comparably passive procedure that does not require movement.

Yet, when employing VR in immersive theatre, and it is argued AR, the interaction may be foremost visually experienced through a headset or screen, but only fully realised when that experience is enhanced by the audience's physical interactions with the work. These interactions can range from a simple turn of the head to view alternative positions of the stage/performance space to being harnessed and carried/wheeled through a warehouse as the participant becomes a part of the dramatic action. For Joris, the immersive VR theatre experience is most effective when it aims for the latter, an active audience able to literally move through the performance space and encounter the world simultaneously exploring and inhabiting the real and the virtual.

The alternative, Joris explains, has proven to be less enjoyable, less desirable and less effective for audiences. To put it simply, if an audience is left in a virtual world without the option of movement, it becomes boring, and the participant soon wishes to end the experience. The transactional interactions for immersive experiences, then, are no longer only a vision of horses but an animated representation that can be observed, altered, and perhaps even influenced by the physical movement of the audience participant as they are given the perception of interaction with that virtual object. A perception that is only achievable, to its fullest extent, through the associated movement around/through/alongside the person perceiving it.

Movement – space, location (LBX), and scalability

While movement is established as key to successful audience engagement in immersive VR theatre, early VR technologies, such as static 'cubes' that participants could enter and look around in, offered limited engagement.

Joris explains that while this could be intriguing, the experience of being in a static cube simply left participants asking, "so what? I'm in a cube, great!" This early technology did not provide the necessary feeling of movement within space, an essential component of creating a truly immersive theatrical world with technology.

A significant breakthrough came with the creation of the CAVE (Cave Automatic Virtual Environment), a 3D stereoscopic space that provides participants with the sensation of physical movement within a virtual environment. It took almost a year for CREW to develop their own version, designed specifically for a VR theatre experience, but Joris confirms they eventually succeeded in creating an immersive encounter that felt physically and spatially real. The development of the CAVE illustrated a key realisation for the Company: space is perceived through movement. Therefore, it reinforces that participants must move to truly experience the depth and expansiveness of the virtual world.

By extension, large spaces became crucial for CREW's immersive productions to provide participants with the freedom they needed to achieve the most impactful experience. The shift to larger environments allowed the full potential of immersive VR theatre to be realised. In contrast to early VR experiences that confined participants to small, predefined areas, Joris recalls that new tracking systems were also developed around 2015, allowing for greater freedom of movement. This included the technique of inside-out tracking, a method that uses location-based cameras to track participants' movements within a space without relying on external markers. This innovation reduced the amount of technology required while improving the fluidity of the experience, making it more accessible with less reliance on expensive setups and alleviating some of the need to invent ways to adapt existing technology to the theatrical event, such as fitting computers to wheelchairs so that their VR-enabling equipment could be wheeled around with participants as they explored the space.

The development of location-based experiences (LBX) further advanced the use of space and audience encounters in immersive productions. Joris explains that the prospect of LBX allows creators to move away from large, empty warehouses and instead use existing buildings and other built environments as the stage for their performances. By incorporating the existing architecture of real-world locations, this type of immersive theatre can further explore the boundaries between virtual and physical realities. This approach offers new possibilities for storytelling, as the space itself can be seen to become a kind of participant in the narrative or at least influence how the narrative is told within it. This is nothing new, as site-specific theatre works have been experimenting with these notions for some time (Tompkins, 2012). However, it has taken until now for advancements in the mobility and utility of technology to enable similar explorations of existing environments through immersive VR/AR encounters.

LBX seems to be an ongoing focus for Joris and his team at CREW, presenting yet unknown possibilities for location-based immersive VR theatre. While other technological advancements have been transformative, limitations still exist, particularly when it comes to scaling these experiences for larger audiences. Joris concedes that in many productions, audience size remains restricted by the logistics of creating an immersive environment with VR. For example, one of the largest immersive shows that CREW has produced to date was able to accommodate 55 participants at a time. While impressive for an immersive VR work, it is not quite comparable to a standard theatre auditorium that seats hundreds of audience members.

This limitation on participant numbers highlights an ongoing challenge: how to maintain the intimate, personal nature of immersive VR theatre while expanding audience capacity and, therefore, it is assumed, scalability, and economic viability. Perhaps, through the development of CARL works, where audiences experience the augmentation communally in contrast to a more intimate VR experience, AR can assist in creating immersive environments for larger audiences.

Joris suggests there are other possible solutions in development that could enable larger audiences for immersive VR theatre, and CREW are working on ways to incorporate greater numbers of participants without sacrificing the quality of the experience. Some of these innovations include the use of digital systems that allow for multiple participants to interact with the same virtual space simultaneously, as well as the development of new tracking technologies that enable more participants to move freely within the performance area. However, these solutions are still in development, and the quest for scalability remains a significant focus. There is also the consideration of the individual immersion that seems so critical to this kind of VR theatre. An interesting investigation would be whether group-immersions change, enhance, diminish or impact the theatrical journey when compared to an individual participant in the experience.

Awareness of real and virtual: Mixed realities, inside, and outside worlds

This concept of motion is further elaborated by Joris, who states that it must be accompanied by an awareness – for the participant – that they are moving through the real world at the same time as they are perceptibly moving through CREW's virtual environment. The combining of real and virtual spaces is often described as mixed reality (Benford & Giannachi, 2008, 2011; Jaller & Serafin, 2020, p. 214). The notion of inhabiting the real and virtual, and the potential for simultaneous motion through both, is crucial to the work of CREW. The dramaturgical unpacking of the company's central understanding of mixed realities as something that must coexist to create a successful immersive experience, rather than a participant's complete immersion in the virtual, has been detailed before (Morin, 2019).

For Joris, immersive VR theatre operates within two simultaneous worlds: the 'inside' world, where the audience is embedded in the action, and the 'outside' world, where spectators may observe from a distance. It is noted that this occurs and the awareness exists in real-time, demonstrating the importance of liveness to this kind of immersive theatre, in the same way it is integral to the theatre experience generally. Both the inside and outside worlds, Joris explains, can have an impact and theatrical function, with those immersed in the experience influenced and affected by that, but also the potential for an audience to observe the participant.

The external audience is also impacted and influenced by the experience, but not in the same way as if they were the ones immersed. They may, for example, be encouraged to consider the experience the participant is having and any ethical, social, or cultural implications associated with their voyeuristic role in the event. Those observing may also be led to consider the thematic explorations of the work, but by virtue of witnessing the participant experience and evolution as a result of those themes, rather than being directly impacted by the evolutionary aspect of the immersive experience themselves.

For the work to have the greatest impact, both kinds of audience – participant and observer – must be aware of the duality of worlds. While the participant is immersed in the VR experience and an active part of its telling, the audience as spectator is more akin to a traditional theatre audience, yet still a part of the experience. Each is active in the duality, but for the audience as participants, the effect of that duality is most impactful when they maintain an awareness that they exist simultaneously in the real and virtual worlds. As Joris explains, the participant must have one foot in each world: they must be aware of their body, to have an out-of-body experience. This is noted by Joris as crucial to provide an effective immersive theatre encounter when using VR technologies.

To consider the audience as participants further, Joris argues that if they are simply sitting or doing nothing, the immersive world loses its dynamism. Passive participation is not engaging; thus, the artist must actively engage the audience by interacting with them, whether through real or simulated displacement: both considered to be expressions of movement. Joris explains that the engagement also extends beyond the physical movement and interaction, with manipulation of the audience's sense of self, reality, and even memory presenting as possibilities for maintaining an active, in-motion experience. The notions of active and movement, then, are broad and encompass not only the requirement for physical motion but also potentially activating elements of the participant's psychological and intellectual processes.

Altering awareness and perception: Psychological motion

CREW have worked closely with this idea that there must also be activation of the participant's mind. In some productions, the illusion of interacting with others was achieved when, in fact, participants were engaging with themselves. The audience's physical movement and simultaneous conscious interaction with the physical space, while maintaining cognisance of their presence in the virtual, remain central to this kind of experience. Anchoring a participant in the here and now while allowing their perception of reality to shift by insinuating a sense of psychological displacement – the feeling of interacting with another – when in fact they have been alone in the virtual with themselves the whole time.

Joris indicates that experiments with the concept of motion, both physical and psychological – the perception of moving oneself/one another through virtual manipulations – not only enhance the audience encounter but also open the dramatic form to an even deeper thematic exploration of the human condition. CREW have demonstrated that conceptualising the use of immersive technologies in this way is a successful method to explore deeper psychological themes, such as memory loss or dementia. This is also the kind of interactivity suggested in the therapeutic application of the arts-based clinical intervention, *Alex*, noted in the chapter above. Similarly in that example, AR effects were combined with audience agency to interact with and move those animations by way of moving their own bodies, enabling a psychological experience previously unknown to them.

Further exemplified in CREW's 2008 work, *W (Double U)*, participants were challenged to experience the world through another person's eyes, in what was described as "head swap technology" (Merx, 2015, p. 204), which on Joris's estimation had a significant impact on the audience. This was a continuation of earlier works, such as *Crash*, which were shown to support the belief that significant audience impact/evolution was achieved through the manipulation of the participant's physical and psychological notions of movement.

At least one critic, Geert Sels, of the Flemish paper *De Standaard*, agrees with this estimation, labelling the production and the work of CREW "ahead of its time," enabling audiences to "feel more than we thought we could" and concluding "Je est un autre" (Sels cited by CREW in: Vanhoutte, 2019). This may be understood as a reference to the Arthur Rimbaud quote, sometimes interpreted to mean that the conception we have of ourselves is not the same as our true self – but also relevant is its literal translation into English: I am the other. Overall, by harnessing the concept of movement and exchanging the psychological sense of self, CREW were able to create an experience that gave the perception of a body-swap: something that is arguably not possible through traditional theatre means without the assistance of immersive technologies.

The great triumph of this kind of work, then, is the way in which it enables audience participants to achieve the feeling of experiencing the world how another might experience it, as close as is conceivably possible. Contrast this with traditional, passive theatre works, which can elicit empathy for and with the circumstances of others – generally represented through characters – it arguably cannot replicate the same depth of experience if the ability to 'feel' and/or 'perceive' the world as if you were someone else is understood to be a deeper experience. The contrast here is not a judgement on the impact or perceived quality of either traditional or VR immersive theatre; it is simply an observation of the differences between audience impact and how encounters facilitated by immersive technologies can deepen participant evolution.

To achieve the greatest audience evolution, immersive theatre must connect with the most profound elements of the human experience – physical, emotional, and intellectual. The audience is invited to explore not just the space but their own identity and perception within it. This interplay with self-perception highlights the psychological and emotional layers of well-constructed and successfully executed immersive theatre. The examples of CREW, reinforce the consideration that adopting immersive technologies can further heighten the effectiveness of the theatrical event in promoting emotional, physical and/or intellectual stimulation, subsequently resulting in significantly enhanced evolutionary change amongst audiences.

Conscious immersion – Resisting flawless illusions

A hallmark of a CREW production is the belief that to fully benefit from an immersive encounter, the participant must remain conscious of their own physical presence. Joris further emphasises that the experience of being inside the immersive world is not about maintaining a perfect illusion but about creating a balance between reality and the theatrical or virtual environment. CREW's approach to illusion in immersive theatre diverges from that of traditional theatre or even film, which Joris posits maintains what he identifies as a Wagnerian model: the illusion must be seamless, with an ideal-stage world separated from the reality of everyday life, often with all stage mechanics hidden to sustain the audience's encapsulation in the fantasy. The machinery of the stage becomes invisible, and the audience is encouraged to forget they are in a theatre.

Similarly, for Joris, in mainstream film, the goal is often to create a perfect illusion that entirely immerses the viewer – so that they cannot turn away from the screen, believing that illusion needs to be perfect; otherwise, the audience will be taken out of it. Yet, CREW's examples of immersive theatre reject this complete submersion into illusion. Similarly to other forms of contemporary performance practice, such as Brechtian theatre or poor theatre, the mechanics are rendered visible, and the audience is purposefully aware that they are a part of a staged event and of the inner workings and mechanics that enable its delivery.

This openness disrupts the idea that the technological illusion for a theatrical experience must be flawless, which seems to contradict the findings of the project discussed in the previous chapter, *Alex: A play with holograms*. For *Alex*, the audience was very sensitive to any imperfections in the augmentations and indicated a preference for more seamless integration of the animated elements. Perhaps this is one point of distinction between the VR works of CREW, and an AR work such as *Alex*. Where audiences of VR should be aware of the effect, perhaps audiences of AR require a different consideration. Perhaps this highlights the different requirements depending on the form. Where a VR immersive experience requires audiences to enter the virtual world, for a CARL experience the augmentation enters the real world. So, when the human enters the virtual world, they must maintain a separation and awareness between the virtual and real; however, when the virtual enters the real world, it should be done as flawlessly as possible.

There is a further distinction between immersive theatre using AR/VR technologies and simply theatre using AR/VR technologies. Perhaps the most obvious explanation for the differences in findings between these examples from CREW and *Alex*, is that the former is very clearly an immersive work, and the latter is simply an AR play. While the use of the technology itself may not require the same considerations around audience awareness, how the technology is embedded in the experience and the aims of using that technology do. Effective immersive theatrical experiences require the awareness that Joris explains, yet a simple AR play may achieve audience satisfaction so long as the effects are believable/do not distract from the experience.

From the works of CREW, we can learn that in immersive environments, illusion plays a role, but the aim is not total immersion where the boundaries between the real and the virtual disappear. Instead, effective immersive theatre keeps these boundaries discernible. In part, this approach grants participants agency, allowing them to move fluidly between reality and the created world, whether that is literally or in their mind: I know I am in an empty room, but I am going to reach out for this virtual prop anyway. The participants are not meant to be entirely consumed by the virtual, but to remain grounded with "one foot in reality," as Joris describes it.

This distinction is critical – immersive experiences should not strive to perfect the illusion; rather, they should engage with the participant's consciousness and agency, inviting them to explore both worlds.

Joris suggests that one of the pitfalls in certain examples of commercial VR experiences, and some theatrical productions, is the attempt to replicate the seamless illusion of mainstream cinema, for example. He argues that commercial VR theatre projects sometimes strive for perfect illusion, as if audiences are watching a virtual film, leaving participants with a 'wow' factor – only to later realise they were not truly part of the experience, merely observers.

Afterwards, Joris explains that audiences can say "Ah! I really wasn't there?!" But then offers the further consideration: "what's the point of that? That's not the point of theatre." This arguably superficial approach contrasts with immersive theatre's deeper intention. Theatre, at its core, should not merely provide a spectacular or entertaining experience: it must provoke emotional or intellectual evolution for the audience. This distinction resonates with the ideas of scholars like Machon (2013) and White (2012), noted above, who argue that immersive theatre should enact a transformative and evolutionary effect, beyond the gimmickry of spectacle.

For Joris, pure illusion can lead to a situation where the physical body of the participant is forgotten, diminishing the transformative power of the experience. In VR theatre, movement is essential: without it, the participant is simply watching, akin to a passive film viewer. The experience is further heightened when the participant actively and knowingly moves through the space, interacting with both the physical and virtual environments. This notion of movement within immersive theatre, and that the audience must be aware of the fact they are involved in a virtual illusion as part of the journey, has connections with another fundamentally accepted component of contemporary performance: Brecht's notion of the verfremdungseffekt.

The very act of enrolling immersive technologies and ensuring audiences are aware of both the technology and their dual existence in the physical and virtual is recognisable as a device to promote a verfremdungseffekt within an immersive theatre experience. By involving the participant in the process of creating or interpreting the narrative, immersive theatre fosters a sense of awareness and cognisant agency, encouraging reflection and change. This further enables theatre makers to explore such complex and political subjects as experiencing the world from another person's point of view.

Immersion and catharsis: Change and liveness as crucial

There are also connections drawn between this notion of audience evolution and change and the inherent association of theatre to Aristotle's concept of catharsis, where the audience undergoes a purging of emotions through engagement with the story. The catharsis is not necessarily provoked by the experiences the audience is shown by virtue of the character and story onstage, however, but is resulting from the immersive experience of the audience member as part of the narrative event themselves and, in the case of *Crash*, the realisation that reality is subjective and that individual experiences are multitudinous. This concept can also be connected to Plato's idea that storytelling holds the power to shape society. By involving the audience in the narrative process, immersive theatre takes on a deeper pedagogical role, guiding participants towards new insights about themselves and the world.

The incorporation of technology to enhance the immersive theatre experience, then, also enhances the fundamental Aristotelean and Platonist components of theatre. This is further argument for immersive works like those of CREW to be seen squarely as acts of theatre, more so than any virtual game world. The experience is not about creating a perfect illusion but about facilitating personal and collective transformation. Indeed, as also discussed by Joris, a perfect, virtual illusion can dissipate the overall effectiveness of the experience, circumventing the requirement for participants to be aware of the real and virtual worlds that they inhabit.

While technology plays an essential role in VR theatre, it is crucial to recognise that theatre, at its core, is a social and human experience which happens in real time. Compared to film or TV, which can be distributed to audiences globally without the need for live actors, theatre relies on the presence of performers and the live interaction between the audience and the world of the play. Joris supports the belief that this social dimension is the reason theatre has endured despite the advent of cinema, television, and other forms of entertainment that do not require live performance.

Immersive theatre, enhanced by AR/VR, amplifies this social experience by placing the audience at the centre of the action. However, it also retains the essential elements of live performance. The creators of immersive theatre, such as CREW, emphasise that the encounters must always be live. Joris explains they consciously avoid creating downloadable experiences, as they believe the essence of theatre lies in its immediacy and the shared encounter of being physically present in the space with others. This insistence on liveness distinguishes their works of theatre from other purely digital or virtual creative expressions.

Lessons for the future

Joris explains that, over time, the lesson has been learnt that less can be more when it comes to creating VR experiences, which can be impacted by sensory overload. Experimental productions from the advent of the technology may have relied heavily on rapid effects and overwhelming stimuli, but it quickly became clear to CREW that a slower, more deliberate pace allows for deeper engagement by the audience. In both immersive theatre and virtual reality, the act of immersion is not about the perfect replication of reality but about creating a space where participants can move between the real and the virtual: the inside and the outside worlds.

The experience becomes transformative when the audience is given the agency to explore their own perceptions, memories, and emotions within the context of the narrative. Immersive theatre, adjacent to Aristotle's catharsis and much like Brecht's alienation, is less concerned with the seamlessness of the illusion and more focused on the audience's intellectual, psychological, and emotional engagement. By blending reality with illusion and inviting active participation by enhancing the opportunities for physical interaction and movement, these experiences are heightened and have the potential to leave a lasting impact on audiences.

The intersection of digital technology and live performance is now an established site of experimentation in contemporary theatre, yet it maintains significant challenges. One of the most critical considerations is how to successfully merge the two realities inherent in these productions: the physical world of the stage and the digital world created by video, 3D animation, VR or AR effects. Joris admits that early experiments integrating these elements in the mid-1990s, were often met with critical resistance. Despite the promise of new technologies, early efforts were labelled by critics as 'interesting failures.' These failures, however, became crucial learning experiences, revealing that the key to success lies in achieving a functional and discernible fusion between digital and live performance, where the audience can move fluidly between the two realities without the cognitive dissonance that can result when the virtual does not align with the physical experience.

If AR technology, for instance, is to be adopted into live theatre performances with the same success and impact as VR has by companies like CREW, then decisions must be made about the purpose of that adoption. Where immersive experiences are the desire, then the concept of motion and how it can be achieved alongside the technology must be contemplated and arguably incorporated into the experience for participants. This notion of movement should not be limited to the physical, but also applied to the more conceptual opportunities for moving, altering and transferring the intellectual and psychological states and awareness of audiences. Furthermore, the place of technology in immersive theatre's future success will depend on its ability to enhance and complement the form as a live, social experience that engages participants emotionally, intellectually, and physically.

Further experiments must be made to investigate how AR and even AI technology can advance these kinds of conceptual explorations of immersive environments, enhancing or evolving elements such as movement and awareness as part of the theatrical experience. The early lessons learnt from the application of VR can be applied to other technologies: resisting the urge to generate perfect digital illusions that rely on rapid effects and over-whelming stimuli in favour of a more measured application of the technology focusing on the thematic exploration and audience evolution in contrast to the gimmickry of the effect.

Adaptability, ingenuity, and invention: Experiences with early adoption of technology in performance

Joris explains that early efforts in creating immersive VR experiences faced numerous challenges due to the limitations of available technology, from cumbersome headsets – which were uncomfortable and unable to produce visuals sufficient for a theatrical experience – to inadequate tracking systems, which lagged or were unable to maintain the pace of the narrative. Generating the VR effects also required unwieldly computing equipment, static cameras and tracking devices, that were limited in terms of participant mobility and interaction. Off-the-shelf equipment was either prohibitively expensive, due to the reliance on complex computer modelling and high-end gear, or within financial reach but inadequate for project ambitions. For these reasons, CREW began experimenting with various combinations of cameras and trackers, eventually developing custom systems. These innovations allowed for more dynamic interaction within the virtual world, enhancing the immersive quality of the experience and enabling more successful theatrical outcomes.

At the outset, productions attempted to incorporate digital elements on traditional stages. For CREW, these early experimentations, often inspired by collaborations with traditional theatre companies, blended live performance with digital projections and video work. However, Joris notes limitations in the ability for these theatres and experiences to allow for full immersion, with much of this early work relying on video and two-dimensional digital media projected/played onstage but not necessarily enabling meaningful audience participation. Placing aside the additional complications with achieving an immersive environment, this experience also seems to echo the accounts of staging *Alex*. Joris indicates that this sometimes remained the case even until 2015, when MoCap technology became more accessible and easier to use. As this occurred, productions began incorporating more complex digital environments that not only facilitated but also required real-time interaction. This shift allowed a greater number of makers the opportunity for departure from traditional stage mechanics when incorporating digital media and video elements towards fully immersive, interactive spaces.

Initially, rather than using the bulky and cumbersome VR headsets that were available for commercial use, CREW engineers adapted a brand of goggles that were developed for use in the home, designed for consumers to watch effects on their televisions. Although not intended for live theatrical experiences, these adapted goggles were more effective, as they were lighter than the heavy-duty commercial equipment, which meant users could wear them for longer periods of time before becoming fatigued. Overcoming some of the limitations of the wearable headsets was only part of the challenge.

The need to maintain audience mobility within the performance space was also critical, leading CREW to experiment with other solutions, such as using wheelchairs to carry computers around behind participants. Adapting these mobility aids enabled CREW staff to follow participants with the processing power needed to generate the virtual effect and maintain the audience's freedom of movement as much as possible. These makeshift systems provided the flexibility required to ensure participants could move freely while remaining connected to the digital environment. Early iterations, though limited, reinforced the ongoing realisation of the importance of movement in immersive experiences and laid the groundwork for more sophisticated systems designed with this in mind.

CREW's early forays into combining the craft of theatre with digital animation were groundbreaking in their ambition, yet notably still discovering the most effective way to unify the two forms. In these early works, Joris explains, the physical reality of the actors on stage and the digital reality of the animation existed as separate, competing worlds. The result was a disjointed experience for the audience, who found it difficult to reconcile the live, tangible presence of actors with the artificial, screen-based environments created by digital animation. As CREW and their collaborators reflected on these works, they came to understand that this disjunct stemmed from the difficulty to fuse these two realities into a cohesive whole.

A cohesive whole, it should be understood, is not the same as a seamless experience, which has already been established as less desirable when generating an effective immersive theatre work with these technologies. In traditional theatre, the stage represents a single, continuous reality. Even when fantastical or abstract elements are introduced – arguably as in a CARL play where the effects are embedded within the staged reality – they operate within the established conventions of live dramatic performance. However, Joris notes, when video or digital elements are added, a new reality is introduced, one that can disrupt the immediacy of the theatrical experience. The audience's cognitive shift between watching a live actor and engaging with a screen creates a disconnect, making it difficult for the two realities to coexist harmoniously.

Technology as prosthesis

A key insight from these early attempts was the understanding that the VR digital elements need to be integrated into the performance in a way that makes them feel like a natural extension of the live world, but not necessarily a seamless part of the live world. The analogy Joris uses to describe this challenge is that of a prosthetic limb: when a prosthetic becomes so well integrated that the user is no longer consciously aware of it, it becomes a natural part of the body. However, the ability to acknowledge and/or understand that it is a prosthetic and an extension of the body, as it were, remains. Similarly, the goal of integrating digital elements in immersive theatre should be to reach a point where the audience may no longer be consciously aware of the divide between the digital and the live, but can choose to acknowledge there is a divide, allowing both to exist as part of a unified, collective reality. The effect must always be balanced with the awareness of the participant's existence of the two worlds, real and virtual.

Joris's experimentation with the fusion of digital and live elements and their conceptual relationships with prosthetics, eventually took on new dimensions through multimedia projects aimed at exploring the embodied experiences of individuals living with disabilities. One such project, *Icarus/Man-O-War* starring paralysed actor Paul Antipoff, involved using VR to simulate the experience of a quadriplegic, providing an opportunity for the audience to 'become' part of a prosthetic machine – a computer-mediated body. This use of VR not only deepened the connection between the physical and digital realms but also offered a new perspective on how technology can expand the range of human experience. In this way, digital tools in immersive theatre can act as a literal prosthesis, enhancing the audience's ability to inhabit new perspectives and experiences, such as simulating to some extent inhabiting a different body. This would be an admirable endeavour to also pursue through the enrolment of AR technologies in live performances. One interesting point of investigation may be to examine whether immersive AR theatre can elicit the same kind of relationship with a virtual prosthetic as the immersive VR work has demonstrated.

The metaphor of multimedia as a prosthesis underscores the potential for digital elements in theatre to enhance, rather than compete with or undermine, live performance. In this framework, digital technology is not simply an external tool, but an extension of the performer's, or audience's, body and the theatrical environment. The challenge is to create an accepted integration where the digital and the live are not experienced as two distinct realms but as a unified, cohesive whole. This notion of fusion – where the digital and physical work with one another – can be seen to mirror advances in prosthetic technology, where users report feeling that their prostheses are extensions of their own bodies, yet consciously aware that they are separate.

In immersive VR theatre, and by extension its AR counterpart, the moment the audience is no longer aware of the 'theatrical machine/mechanics' – the video projections, AR/VR digital animations – as separate or invasive elements in their world is when the fusion of virtual and real worlds occurs. At this point, the mechanical/digital and the embodied can coexist without tension, and the audience can fully inhabit the world of the performance.

Perhaps this was the issue with the complete audience acceptance of the augmentations in *Alex*. The problem was not with the creation of a seamless, or otherwise, digital augmentation. The impediment was with the fact that the failings of the animation led to an effect that seemed to exist within its own realm, rather than part of the unified, whole realm of the world of the play. The shortcomings in the animation programming, not being anchored properly to the horizontal axis that mimicked the literal placement of the stage floor, meant it appeared separate from the world of the play, existing along a different spatial plane from the rest of the stage and performers.

Experiments with telepresence and gaming

Other preliminary works of CREW demonstrate different tensions that had to be overcome when adapting new technologies into live theatre. Telepresence, a concept explored in Joris's early experiments, involves the idea of being present in a space through digital mediation, such as video feeds or virtual environments. In these productions, telepresence allows the audience to experience different realities simultaneously – both the live action of the stage and the remote or virtual worlds created by technology. However, these experiments were initially seen as failures by Joris because the two realities could not be reconciled. The audience experienced a jarring shift between the live actors and the digital representations, which prevented the necessary fusion of worlds.

Deconstructed games were another element CREW's early work engaged with. These experiments played with the interactive and rule-bound nature of games, challenging traditional notions of storytelling in theatre. While deconstructing game logic offered new possibilities for audience interaction, it also highlighted the complexity of merging interactive, rule-based digital environments with the fluid, unpredictable nature of live performance. Just as in their work with digital animation on a traditional theatre stage, the challenge to create a smooth transition between the two worlds – the game and the play – hindered the audience's ability to engage with the performance as a cohesive whole.

A summary to this section

For CREW, much of their evolution with immersive theatre and VR has been driven by the need to overcome technological limitations and expand the possibilities of audience engagement. From the early days of adapting consumer electronics to the development of complex but more mobile motion capture and tracking systems, these creators have consistently pushed the boundaries of what is possible. The emphasis on space and movement as fundamental components of immersion has shaped the design and execution of these productions, ensuring that participants are not just passive observers but active in the narrative. Yet, the question of how to fuse digital and live realities remains constant. CREW's early attempts revealed that the primary challenge lies not in the technology itself but in how it is used to enhance the live experience rather than detract from it. To overcome this, theatre makers must develop a new theatrical language – one that can articulate the relationship between the digital and the embodied in ways that audiences can intuitively understand and engage with.

As technology continues to advance, the potential for even more immersive, large-scale experiences will grow. LBX and innovations in tracking systems are already moving the field in new directions, allowing creators to more easily use real-world environments as part of their storytelling. The future of immersive theatre lies in its ability to merge the virtual with the physical, providing audiences with experiences that challenge their perceptions of space, self, and reality. As these technologies become more accessible, the potential for immersive AR/VR theatre to reach broader audiences while maintaining its transformative power will only increase.

CREW have demonstrated that the continued adoption of these evolving technologies – from VR to AR and beyond – requires makers to adapt, reengineer and invent ways for the technology to meet the needs of dramatic storytelling. Theatre doers cannot simply wait for the technology to adapt to their needs. The fusion of digital and live performance is not merely a technical challenge but a philosophical one. It requires creators to think deeply about the nature of reality, embodiment, and perception. As immersive theatre that relies on these technologies continues to push the boundaries of what is possible, the goal will be to create experiences where digital technology is not an external intrusion but an integrated part of the theatrical world – where there may be a perceptible divide between the two, but the audience experiences them as one unified reality.

Specialisation, collaboration, audience, and artist evolution: Other considerations when using new technologies in theatre

The integration of cutting-edge technology into theatre presents new possibilities for creating theatrical experiences, but it also presents significant challenges, particularly for those who lack access, knowledge, and skills to use the technology. This kind of theatre demands more than the conventional skill sets of actors and directors, for example: it requires a hybrid team that may include computer technicians, engineers and developers, animators and digital designers, and theatrical storytellers capable of bridging the gap between technological innovation and audience engagement. These multidisciplinary teams must develop not only the technical infrastructure but also the creative language needed for them to communicate and to utilise and sustain these emerging forms of theatre.

For CREW, their collaborative teams most often include a combination of technologists and artists working closely. This comprises technical specialists such as engineers, programmers, and developers. The complexity of integrating VR, MoCap tracking systems and other advanced technologies into live performances requires highly skilled professionals. However, Joris stresses that these technicians must also possess creative sensibilities to collaborate effectively in a theatrical context. By the same token, Joris cautions that traditional theatre practitioners, exemplified in actors accustomed to performing dialogue for passive audiences, may find immersive environments challenging or even frustrating if they are not open to engaging with the technical elements of the production. For this reason, while it is useful for technologists and engineers to possess at least an interest in creativity and art, it is also desirable for the artists to hold a curiosity for the technological.

The need for multi-disciplinary expertise with at least an interest in the creative and technological elements involved cannot be overstated. Storytellers, actors, and directors must understand, at least at a rudimentary level, the technical aspects of VR/AR immersive theatre to fully exploit its potential. The audience of immersive theatre does not sit passively, waiting for the narrative to unfold; they are active participants, often leading the action themselves. Actors, for example, may need to adjust their expectations of performance, recognising that their role is also to facilitate participant engagement rather than simply deliver a pre-scripted performance or, to put it bluntly, take the spotlight while an adoring audience sits and basks in their theatrical delivery. Further, Joris explains that the shared understanding and interest for all elements of the form must go beyond the relationships between those who create the work, extending to those who produce and programme the experience.

Joris articulates that a common frustration for creators working with technology is the disconnect with creative venue programmers that can sometimes arise, with tech-creatives and producers often approaching the art form from different perspectives. Theatre programmers may ask questions, such as "What is it about?" – questions grounded in traditional storytelling forms that may not apply in an immersive VR/AR experience context, where the answer may be: "it is about the audience experience." From a traditional theatre producers' perspective, this may seem hard to promote – or sell – and might not fit with the established image they perceive their venue, or festival, to have and the kinds of works it is expected to produce. This disconnect can hinder the creative process, as techno-immersive theatre practitioners often seek to move beyond conventional narrative structures to create experiences that explore space, movement, and interaction. The form is still in flux, and much of its future success depends on developing a shared language not only between the creative and technical teams, but also between the project team and arts administration, who are key in providing opportunities for the form to develop and grow.

Furthermore, it is suggested that a critical obstacle to the further development of VR/AR and similar technologies in theatre is a lack of suitable performance spaces – spaces designed specifically for this kind of performance. Immersive VR experiences as described above, particularly, require environments that are flexible and spacious enough to accommodate movement, tracking technologies, and interactive design elements. Arguably, the same requirements could support AR technologies to create immersive environments as well.

Traditional theatres, with their fixed seating and proscenium stages, are often ill-suited to immersive productions in general, let alone if those productions also require specialist equipment to be installed. This is one of the infrastructural obstacles to production success highlighted in the CARL experience detailed in the previous chapter. However, investment in conventional theatre spaces seems to be a default in many jurisdictions, limiting the potential for new types of theatre to evolve on its own terms. Admittedly, the point made by Joris above regarding the evolution of LBX and technologies that are increasingly able to facilitate site-specific works may operate to overcome some of these tensions.

To fully realise the possibilities of this kind of theatre, Joris suggests that new types of performance spaces should be developed. The desire is for these spaces to be adaptable, large, and capable of integrating advanced technologies such as AR, VR, and motion tracking. Joris confirms that future-ready, technology-enabled theatres would allow creators to experiment with new forms of storytelling that are not confined by the limitations of traditional stage mechanics, nor hindered by the additional consideration of how to make the technology function at its peak within a space not specifically designed for it to work. Although, any transition to tailored performance spaces requires significant support that is not only financial, but also institutional and cultural – there must be some kind of social agreement between artists, funders, governments, and audiences that increasingly scarce resources may, at least in part, be redirected into new ways of making theatre arts.

Despite the strong history of immersive theatre achieved through VR technologies, Joris concludes, it is still an evolving artistic form, in the early stages of its development as the technology also develops. The technical language and practices needed to communicate between creators, technologists, and producers/programmers are still evolving. For Joris, this is analogous to the early days of cinema, where filmmakers experimented with narrative forms and technological processes before arriving at the now-established conventions, techniques and creative and practical lexicon that defines the form and enables it to function within its own accepted ecology.

In the same way that the language of filmmaking developed over time – moving from static camera shots to complex, dynamic cinematography – VR/AR theatre also needs time to experiment and refine its own techniques. One of the key insights from CREW's early attempts is the need for experimentation not only to discover *how* to make the technology work but also to understand *why* it works and how audiences respond to it. This process is crucial to developing the grammar and syntax of technology-facilitated immersive theatre, allowing for the accepted integration of digital and live elements. Joris implores that this kind of theatre must be allowed to grow through a similar period of experimentation to that of film. This creative process will also reveal where it fits within the broader theatrical and artistic spectrum, whereafter it will be possible to identify how it can be utilised to its greatest effect.

Joris also notes that across the previous two decades, while technology and understandings of how it can be embedded within live performance experiences have changed, audience behaviour has also evolved, particularly in response to immersive theatre. Joris reflects, looking back over the form's early experiments in immersive environments, audiences were often left confused, unsure and possibly unconfident of how to interact with the space. Audience members, especially those experienced with a traditional theatre show, expected a passive experience in which something happened to them, rather than feeling immediate permission to do things to/explore the space. However, as immersive experiences have become more widespread and digital technology in general has become more commonplace in people's everyday lives, audiences have begun to understand that they must actively participate. Today, Joris confirms that many audience members instinctively know that they need to move, explore, and engage with the environment for the experience to unfold fully.

However, the point is made that the technology should only be deployed in consideration of the audience's capacity to accept it. Despite the rapid evolution and ever-growing awareness of audience familiarity with immersive and other technologies, Joris warns that creators must remain mindful of the audience's limitations. Immersive experiences cannot advance faster than audiences are willing to accept. In the early days of immersive theatre, Joris admits that some of CREW's experiments were fascinating to the creators but left audiences bewildered. This disconnect highlights the importance of pacing the evolution of the form to ensure that audiences remain engaged and do not feel estranged or disaffected by the technology, nor confused by its place within their experience. Makers must strike a balance between pushing the boundaries of the form and providing encounters that audiences can comprehend and enjoy.

As VR/AR theatre continues to develop, the challenge will be to balance technological innovation with the preservation of theatre's fundamental social and human qualities. The form must evolve through collaboration between creative, technical and administrative professionals, with a shared understanding and interest in both the artistic and technological elements involved. Reinforcing arguments around considerations of infrastructure, new performance spaces must be designed to accommodate the needs of immersive experiences created with technology, allowing the form to grow. The challenge for creators will be to continue pushing the boundaries of what is possible in hybrid digital environments while ensuring that the audience remains at the heart of the experience so that the practice can cultivate in alignment with them. By supporting the form with its own period of evolutionary development, this kind of theatre can be established as a distinct and enduring practice within dramatic arts more broadly that harnesses the power of both technology and theatre's poetics as a powerful expression of the human condition.

Concluding with a dramaturgical framework for creating immersive theatre with AR/VR technology

Joris explains that the integration of digital and physical experiences in immersive VR theatre, particularly, requires a careful and deliberate approach to dramaturgy: one that considers not only the narrative and technical aspects but also the audience's physical and emotional well-being. In immersive environments, especially those incorporating VR, and presumably AR, through headsets, headphones and other wearables, harnesses and other sensory tools that alter the audience's perception of reality, Joris cautions that participants can experience disorientation, confusion and anxiety, as well as sometimes associated physical symptoms such as nausea and dizziness.

To address these challenges, the dramaturgical process must include strategies that guide participants seamlessly into and out of the immersive world, ensuring their comfort and safety throughout the experience. Jaller and Serafin describe this as "transition design to secure experience continuity"

(2020, p. 1). For theatre makers, this can be considered an element of the dramaturgical design, extending beyond shaping the story or the performance to developing a process that allows participants to physically and emotionally navigate the experience. Below is a summary of how Joris describes the dramaturgy of CREW and the way it addresses the unique demands of immersive theatre achieved through technology, focusing on techniques used to manage physical discomfort and emotional transitions for the audience.

The transition into the immersive world must be handled with care. CREW productions may begin by gently guiding participants into the environment, allowing them to adjust to the sensory changes at their own pace. A key aspect of this dramaturgy is preparing the audience for the physical experience. For instance, in some productions, audiences are given headphones to help them focus and block out external stimuli. However, wearing headphones while navigating an unfamiliar space can be disorienting. To mitigate this, as part of enrolment in the performance, participants are taught how to move and walk while wearing headphones, ensuring that they feel comfortable and secure before entering the immersive environment. This gradual process allows audience members to acclimate to the technology and the unique physical demands of the experience.

In productions where participants are suspended in harnesses to simulate flying/floating, the dramaturgy includes a slow, step-by-step process to bring them into this new physical state. This might begin with small, familiar actions – such as walking into the performance space – before gradually introducing more complex physical sensations, like the feeling of weightlessness in a harness. By slowly easing participants into these sensations and embedding the enrolment into the dramaturgy of the theatrical world, the process helps reduce anxiety and discomfort, allowing for a more integrated immersion. This dramaturgical approach – embedding the enrolment process into the experience – also includes constant communication with the participants, which helps maintain their sense of orientation and safety.

Talking to participants throughout the journey, particularly when they are about to engage in physically or emotionally intense activities, CREW has found it can help mitigate feelings of disorientation. For example, as participants are brought into the harnesses that will lift them off the ground, they are spoken to and reassured. This verbal connection grounds the participants, reminding them that they are still in control of their bodies, even as they are lifted into an unfamiliar physical sensation. This also reaffirms the awareness component of the immersive experience, leveraging the requirement for participants to be aware that they are indeed inhabiting the inner and outer worlds simultaneously.

Equally important to the dramaturgical design of this kind of encounter is how participants are guided out of the virtual. Just as they are slowly introduced to the world of the performance, they must also be carefully brought back to reality. Joris describes, in some productions, this transition is symbolised by a return to daylight or a moment where the participants reconnect with another person. For instance, after being suspended in a harness, participants are gently lowered and reintroduced to a shared physical space where they encounter an actor who gives them a welcoming smile – often the first thing they see upon re-entry into the real world. This human connection helps reorient participants, grounding them emotionally and physically after the disorienting experience of weightlessness during virtual immersion.

The dramaturgical process always includes a clear and intentional method for entering and exiting the immersive world. These transitions are not abrupt but are designed to guide participants through the shift in realities. By carefully managing how participants exit the immersive space, creators help alleviate any lingering feelings of disorientation or discomfort, ensuring that the experience remains safe from beginning to end.

A further tangential but nonetheless important aspect related to audience experience, embedded within CREW's works, is the frequent incorporation of external perspectives. For example, cameras may be used to capture what participants are experiencing in real-time, allowing others – whether fellow participants or external observers – to see what is happening from an audience member's point of view. This not only creates a sense of shared experience but also provides a way for participants to engage with the performance on multiple levels. While one participant might be experiencing the sensation of flying in a harness or navigating a virtual environment, others can watch through the camera feed, creating a bridge between the immersive and non-immersive components. This camera feed offers a window into the participant's subjective encounter, enhancing the overall performance by expanding the range of perspectives available to multiple audiences.

The dramaturgy of immersive theatre is not just about storytelling. It is about creating a holistic experience that considers the audience's physical, emotional, and sensory journey. In productions that incorporate augmented and/or virtual reality, harnesses, and other immersive technologies, the dramaturgical process must address the potential for discomfort and disorientation. By carefully guiding participants into and out of the immersive world, using techniques such as verbal communication, gradual transitions, and sensory management, creators can ensure that the audience remains comfortable and engaged throughout the experience. Moreover, the use of cameras and external perspectives enhances the sense of shared experience, allowing those outside the virtual environment to participate in the performance in their own way.

The fusion of digital and live performance holds immense potential for the theatrical experience, but it also presents significant challenges. Early experiments like those conducted by Joris and his collaborators were crucial in identifying fundamental obstacles to this fusion and laying the groundwork for them to be overcome. Aligning the dramaturgy to address audience experience as part of the theatrical world is a key component of ensuring a successful immersion with technology. It is only through the safe and considered fusion of the real participant with their augmented/virtual immersive environments that the experience can be leveraged to its greatest potential. This fusion, once achieved, opens new possibilities for storytelling, engagement, and empathy, allowing immersive theatre using emerging technologies to push the boundaries of what it means to experience performance in the digital age.

References

About CREW. (2024). CREW. Retrieved 8 October from https://crew.brussels/en/about-crew

Alston, A. (2013). Audience participation and neoliberal value: Risk, agency and responsibility in immersive theatre. *Performance Research, 18*(2), 128–138. https://doi.org/10.1080/13528165.2013.807177

Benford, S., & Giannachi, G. (2008). Temporal Trajectories in Shared Interactive Narratives. *26th Annual CHI Conference on Human Factors in Computing Systems*, New York, NY, USA.

Benford, S., & Giannachi, G. (2011). *Performing Mixed Reality*. MIT Press.

Bloom, G. (2018). *Gaming the Stage: Playable Media and the Rise of English Commercial Theater*. University of Michigan Press. https://ebookcentral.proquest.com/lib/qut/detail.action?docID=6796730

Giannachi, G. (2004). *Virtual Theatres: An Introduction*. Taylor & Francis Group. https://ebookcentral.proquest.com/lib/qut/detail.action?docID=182374

Jaller, C., & Serafin, S. (2020). Transitioning Into States of Immersion: Transition design of mixed reality performances and cinematic virtual reality. *Digital Creativity, 31*(3), 213–222. https://doi.org/10.1080/14626268.2020.1779091

Kriebel, S. (n.d.). *The Unbuilt Room*. Retrieved 14 October, 2024 from https://www.unbuiltroom.com/about

Machon, J. (2013). *Immersive Theatres: Intimacy and Immediacy in Contemporary Performance*. Red Globe Press. https://search.ebscohost.com/login.aspx?direct=true&AuthType=sso&db=nlebk&AN=1522736&site=ehost-live&scope=site&custid=qut

Mangan, M. (2006). Escape Mechanisms: Smoke, mirrors and the arts of masculinity. In A. Kiernander, J. Bollen, & B. Parr (Eds.), *What A Man's Gotta Do? Masculinities in Performance* (pp. 21–27). University of New England.

Merx, S. (2015). Doing phenomenology the empathetic implications of crew's head-swap technology in 'W' (Double U). In M. Bleeker, J. Foley Sherman, & E. Nedelkopoulou (Eds.), *Performance and Phenomenology: Traditions and Transformations*. Taylor & Francis Group. https://ebookcentral.proquest.com/lib/qut/detail.action?docID=2011215

Morin, J. M. (2019). Réalité virtuelle et alternée dans la pratique de CREW_ERIC JORIS: Mise en oscillation du corps immergé. *Percées* (1–2). https://doi.org/10.7202/1075185ar

Shakespeare, W., Taylor, G., & Ackland, J. (1982). *Oxford Shakespeare: Henry V.* Oxford University Press. https://ebookcentral.proquest.com/lib/qut/detail.action?docID=3055127

Sterling, P., & McAvoy, M. (2017). Art, Pedagogy, and Innovation: Tracing the roots of immersive theatre and practice. In J. Machamer (Ed.), *Immersive Theatre* (pp. 93–108). Common Ground Research Networks. https://search.ebscohost.com/login.aspx?direct=true&AuthType=sso&db=nlebk&AN=1910946&site=ehost-live&scope=site&custid=qut

Tompkins, J. (2012). The 'place' and practice of site-specific theatre and performance. In A. Birch & J. Tompkins (Eds.), *Performing Site-Specific Theatre: Politics, Place, Practice* (pp. 1–17). Palgrave Macmillan UK. https://ebookcentral.proquest.com/lib/qut/detail.action?docID=1058315

Vanhoutte, K. (2019). Lucid dreamers: Immersive re-enactment in the work of CREW. *Archée*(Décembre2019).https://archee.uqam.ca/decembre-2019-lucid-dreamers-immersive-re-enactment-in-the-work-of-crew/index.html

Vanhoutte, K., & Wynants, N. (2011). Performing phenomenology: Negotiating presence in intermedial theatre. *Foundations of Science, 16,* 275–284. https://doi.org/10.1007/s10699-010-9193-8

White, G. (2012). On immersive theatre. *Theatre Research International, 37*(3), 221–235. https://doi.org/10.1017/S0307883312000880

5

CASE STUDY 3: VISIONARY ARTISTS IN SOUTHEAST ASIA

Three examples (plus 1x3) from Singapore, including Tamil language theatre, traversing the arts/tech nexus

In 2014, the Singapore Government initiated a national policy known as the 'Smart Nation' initiative (Sipahi & Saayi, 2024). This has been promoted as a turning point for the city-state, aiming to become a world-first leader in digitisation across all areas of government and society. From business to education and health, the policy champions and promotes the embrace of digital to "overcome various national challenges, improve the quality, efficiency and performance of urban services, sustainable development and overall improvement of citizens' lives" (p. 41). The arts in Singapore are also seen to have embraced this policy focus, with the nation's creative bodies since producing several key industry initiatives aiming to bring the technology and arts disciplines together, encouraging experimentation and investigation between the two sectors.

In 2017, the Infocomm Development Authority of Singapore (IMDA), a statutory body created to develop Singapore as a global information commerce capital (Gary, 2013, p. 11), hosted an inaugural arts and technology festival, the Festival of Technology. This event and its focus on collaboration between art and technology was touted as "expand[ing] the Singapore Smart Nation reach to new audiences" (Ibrahim, 2017). The Singaporean National Arts Council (NAC) is also noted as prioritising the intersection between the arts and technology, since at least 2018, through the 'Our SG Arts Plan' (Liew, 2022). NAC later launched the associated Arts x Tech Lab in 2021, an ongoing initiative described as: "an innovation lab for Singapore's artists to integrate and experiment with digital technology to improve art-making and create new arts experiences for the public" (National Arts Council, 2022).

DOI: 10.4324/9781003521907-5

Singapore, then, is an obvious choice as a focus for a book addressing art and technology. In October 2024, I spent a week in the Lion City, experiencing immersive installations, meeting with local theatre makers and companies, and visiting creative headquarters and studios. This chapter is a reflection on that time spent in Singapore, focusing on interviews conducted with representatives from three, local innovators, experimenting with AR, VR and AI in live performance. They are Saskia Bünte and Ivan Liew, producers from the interactive design and mixed reality experience company, The Doodle People; from the company, AGAM Theatre Lab – responsible for the world's first Tamil language AR play – Founder, Subramanian Ganesh, and Non-Executive Director, Nallu Dhinakharan; and the world-renowned filmmaker, visual artist, and immersive media creator, Ho Tzu Nyen.

I also encountered three separate immersive experiences presented at the ArtScience Museum, located at the integrated resort complex of Marina Bay Sands. This included the augmented reality and projection mapping exhibit, *Future World: Where art meets science*, the virtual reality immersion, *Sen VR*, and the more traditional arts exhibit – consisting of models, replicas, and drawn/painted/sculpted/built installations rather than digital effects immersions – *The World of Studio Ghibli*. These experiences, each exploiting a different kind of immersive format, provide interesting counterpoints to contrast and compare the application of their respective forms. Each example provides provocations and considerations of how its format might be leveraged effectively to generate an impactful experience for theatrical audiences.

While not strictly plays/theatrical works, *Sen VR*, in particular, could be understood to incorporate a dramatic narrative. Regardless, it is hoped all three may provide insight into how theatre might leverage the technology applied in each case to achieve its own aims. This chapter will discuss each of the above-mentioned three focus interviews in turn, before briefly reflecting on the immersive experiences of the ArtScience Museum. As with previous chapters, this section is chiefly a reflection on each of the relevant interviews, traversing between comments, notions, and ideas directly from the contributors, interspersed with my own thoughts and considerations inspired by these conversations. Attribution is given to points provided directly by others; otherwise, the words can be taken as my own general considerations inspired by the interviews, gathered from notes made by me during and after each interaction.

Insights from the engineers: Words from the technologists and producers at The Doodle People, a company responsible for several creative collaborations

The Doodle People are a mixed reality and interactive design company with projects spanning marketing, brand engagement, gaming, and audience interaction – in both the marketing and consumer definition and live performance understanding of the term 'audience.' Driven by CEO Lynette Ee, with leadership also from Creative Technical Director (CTD), Timothi Lim, this is a commercial tech company that has collaborated on some high-impact digital theatre projects. These include the AR works, 拜拜年 *Bai Bai Nian* (*Happy New Year*) and the DOTS project, as well as the international VR experience, *KINetic*. I discussed some of these projects and their personal philosophies around art and technology with two of The Doodle People producers, Saskia Bünte and Ivan Liew, who were gracious enough to meet with me in Ee and Lim's absence. The CEO and CTD, described by their team as enthusiastic patrons of the arts, otherwise engaged during my Singapore field research, at the time conducting exciting projects in Germany and the UK, respectively.

KINetic – A VR experience

Perhaps the most ambitious project in live performance and technology for The Doodle People to date is a VR experience. Presented in 2022, it was a cross-continental production called *KINetic*. Bünte and Liew describe the work as a virtual performance with three dancers, two located in Singapore and another in South Korea. The dancers' movement was tracked using a commercially available system, the HTC Vive Pro, and the online representation was hosted on the digital platform, VRChat. Audience members were able to join the online space from anywhere in the world, logging on to watch the dancers perform through their own, personal virtual headsets. Participants also had the ability to move around the dancing virtual bodies, to view them from any angle while in the virtual world, as well as being able to explore the digital environment more broadly. Dancers were also provided with a headset, so that they could see audience members – represented by their virtual avatars – watching them as the performance unfolded. There were also screens set up for operational staff alongside the dancers so they could view the digital world and what was happening between the digital dancers and audience. *KINetic* was created as part of Pluritopia, a symposium held collaboratively between the Arts Councils of Singapore and Korea.

It may be interesting to discuss this VR work briefly, as a comparative example keenly able to demonstrate some of the distinctions identified in earlier sections of this book, related to the classifications of digital theatre broadly, VR theatre generally and live immersive VR performance specifically. In some ways, *KINetic* supports the advice provided by Joris in the Chapter 4, regarding the key characteristics of live performance works incorporating virtual environments: movement as vital to the encounter. In *KINetic*, the audience could 'move' their digital avatar around the space using a hand-held controller, though their physical body may be in a static position.

This example of movement may be seen in contrast to many of the works of CREW, where participants may also roam freely in their physical world. Further, while there is agency for audiences in *KINetic* to explore the online space, the associated notions of inner and outer worlds are arguably preserved most significantly for the operational staff viewing the screens set up alongside the performers; these staff are able to observe both worlds concurrently. There are differences, then, between this example from The Doodle People and those ascribed to CREW in terms of how motion is applied and the duality of worlds is understood.

For *KINetic* audiences, the movement is largely only in the virtual world as they sit, potentially, at home in their living room chairs, exploring the digital reality through the impression of movement provided by their wearable device. The awareness of the inside – digital – and outside – real – worlds further contrasted to the examples of CREW, with the distinction made obvious for those supporting the production around the performers, but not so intentionally for the audience. Perhaps, then, and to provide a further evidentiary illustration to distinguish between the various forms, *KINetic* may be viewed as an example of digital dance theatre broadly, and arguably a live VR performance experience specifically, but resisting notable facets of VR immersive theatre. As a form, it can be understood to enable physically distanced audiences to attend a production enacted by non-collocated performers, brought together in a virtual world, rather than strictly a VR-enabled immersive theatrical experience, for example.

拜拜年 *Bai Bai Nian (Happy New Year) – An AR experience*

To now focus specifically on the use of AR technology, another work co-created by The Doodle People is 拜拜年 *Bai Bai Nian*. This production premiered at Singapore's Festive Arts Theatre in January 2023, supported by the NAC. In Chinese mythology, Nian is a beast said to have lived below the oceans, venturing to the surface only on the final day of the lunar year, where it would terrorise villages and even eat local inhabitants. One day, a mysterious stranger arrived in one particular village, and some versions of the legend say they were offered refuge by a kindly elder who asked them to help the villagers expel Nian in return for their hospitality (CENFENG, 2023). Another version of the tale sees the stranger take on Nian without this request, the transient figure ultimately proving to be a powerful god in disguise (Tan, 2007). A third account asserts that the villagers enlisted the help of a great lion, who agreed to scare away the beast, but Nian vowed to return at the same time the following year. When the lion refused to help again, the people took it upon themselves to design their own lion costume to fool and scare the beast away (Wu, 2006).

Despite the variations in accounts, all stories are similar in their description of fireworks, drums, and the threatening colours of red being used to intimidate and frighten Nian out of the village, never to return. The story of Nian, then, is the source of the now commonly understood symbols of Lunar New Year celebrations in the Chinese tradition: lion/dragon dancers, red streamers, fireworks, and acrobatic drummers. The Doodle People's all-ages story, 拜拜年 *Bai Bai Nian*, sees the protagonist's distant relative brought from the past to explain the origins of the Chinese New Year celebrations, and together the characters find a way to again defeat a returned Nian monster.

Bünte and Liew explain that AR played a crucial role in bringing the Nian monster to the live stage. The effect was achieved using smartphone filters to overlay the beastly face of Nian atop the real face of an actor, projected onto a screen directly behind the action. In this way, the technology was able to bring the animation of Nian to life in real time, a smartphone setup downstage where the actor could approach and have their face manipulated, 'Nian-ified,' and projected to the onstage backdrop. The animated character was generated in the moment as the action unfolds, capturing the actor's facial expressions and movements for the audience to see, and the other actors to react to, in the full sense of liveness.

This is a similar outcome to that described in the chapter above discussing the AR play, *Alex*, with the augmentation projected in a CARL effect without the need for audiences to use their own wearable or handheld device to perceive the augmentation. The main point of difference being that the Nian augmentation was a facial filter animating the actor's head, while the Alex character was a full-body animation. Further, *Alex* the play used Hologauze equipment to achieve a holographic effect, while 拜拜年 *Bai Bai Nian* utilised traditional projection screens to present the effect as a two-dimensional image as part of the show's video backdrop. It is also noted that it was a chief aim of the *Alex* production to capture the nuanced facial expressions of the actor operating the augmented character, which it failed to do. 拜拜年 *Bai Bai Nian*, on the other hand, seems to have achieved this spectacularly well, applying retail AR programmes altered specifically for the show to achieve an animated-face effect that remained elusive to the *Alex* production team.

Thoughts on collaboration – Passion, shared language, and communication

Regardless of the VR or AR underpinnings of the works, *KINetic* and 拜拜年 *Bai Bai Nian*, it is clear the technological and systems expertise and knowledge of those at The Doodle People were paramount in creating high-quality, impactful creative outcomes. For Bünte and Liew, they see their role as digital technology experts to facilitate live performances, not necessarily as makers. They describe their roles as enablers, rather than artists. Further, the two are unanimous in the belief that passion is crucial for a successful collaboration between theatre-makers and technologists. Liew confirmed that passion is important: "the engineers need a passion and interest in the arts. These projects require a lot of collaborators to make them happen. Artists and engineers must both be interested in the creative side." This is a sentiment echoed in the case studies of previous chapters, continually emerging as a key component of technology-infused theatrical practice.

Bünte further elaborates on the requirement for a shared interest in these collaborative environments. Observing that:

> Often during [these kinds of] projects, frictions develop as each person comes at it from their own discipline's perspective and have different expectations, requirements and things they consider important. There is no shared language, which can make it hard to unify the goal but also to work through any problems. Understanding comes only over time and working with each other on projects more and more.

This notion of shared language also emerges as common across projects attempting to enmesh theatre and new technologies. Here, the astute distinction is made between not only being able to understand and express a unified vision, but also having a shared comprehension to overcome any challenges that emerge on the journey to realising that vision. The inference being, it is not only the shared values and passion for the project and the art, which are also raised as critical to these kinds of collaborations, that are essential to success; if there are issues of communication, this can also lead to moments of failure or complete abandonment of the endeavour overall.

Bünte adds further insight to this thought, confirming that a shared passion should go beyond a general interest in technology and how it might be applied in creative contexts, declaring that there is little purpose to "tech for tech's sake." This can be taken to mean, that any shared interest should extend farther than the fusion of technology and theatre arts, perhaps to the underlying motivation and meaning behind the work itself. The technology should support the aims and intentions of its creators, and work to have a meaningful impact on its audiences. It must not simply be incorporated because it can be incorporated, and developers like Liew and Bünte are able to incorporate it. Therefore, I argue their connection to the work can be seen not just as an enabler or facilitator of the experience from a practical standpoint – the people who help to make the technology work – but also enablers of the creative intentions and the resultant impact it has on audiences. From this perspective, technology producers, like those at The Doodle People, have a defensible role in the future evolution of live performance with technology in the creation of dramatic and other embodied narrative worlds, arguably in much the same way a lighting, sound, set, costume, and vision designer has today.

The creative and commercial imperatives

Interestingly, there was another element to collaboration that entered the discussion with Bünte and Liew. It arose from considerations of the future of these kinds of projects and centred on the commercial imperatives that may also be approached from different angles by the theatre sector, compared to the private tech sector. To be clear, both producers were very supportive of the arts and gave no indication of demanding the further commodification of humanity's artistic expressions. However, in my estimation as someone who has also worked on these projects, there is the potential for artist-creators to approach these kinds of collaborations with the same expectations as they would any work of theatre. Placing aside the comparably healthy profits of commercially produced musical spectacles and the comparatively securely funded works of large publicly subsidised State theatre companies in wealthy jurisdictions, there is no denying that independent theatre the world over relies on volunteer labour, donated time and in-kind support, to operate. For many commercial industries outside of the arts, not just the technology sector, the concept of operating under such economically fragile, and arguably exploitative means, may be difficult to rationalise – and defend to employees, shareholders, and equity partners.

The provocation is, then, that ongoing collaborations between such diverse industries as the creative and the technological should also consider the commercial outcome. To me, this means the creative objectives of the theatre-team should attempt to somehow respond, or at least be sensitive, to the commercial imperatives of their industry collaborators. Otherwise, there is the risk that engineers, digital designers, and animation collaborators may become yet another highly burdened, but under-compensated cog in the theatre machine – a kind of exploitation often treated as normal in the theatre industry, but should be challenged generally and not only when dealing with non-theatre industry partners. This kind of parasitic relationship, where the theatre takes what it needs for its outcome without regard for its collaborative host, will inevitably lead to willing collaborators becoming less and less obliging, potentially derailing the continued and important evolution of theatre and technology.

Bünte points out, though, that in their estimation, collaboration will always continue, as there is "a natural desire for people to collaborate, to do and try something different." Yet, across projects, the obstacles are always the same no matter the sector: "the right people, enough time and sufficient resources." I conclude that this is why initiatives, such as Singapore's Smart Nation, are crucial to the ongoing advancement and survival of cultural heritage. Perhaps for now, it is realistically only with sincere public investment, as well as interest and support from large cultural institutions who may have access to additional resources, such as universities, that these collaborations have a feasible basis for any kind of commercial practicability adequate to maintain healthy industry partnerships. At least until the technology and its theatrical application are more fully understood, the costs are reduced as it becomes more commonplace, and the value of arts to developing technology is also acknowledged, the sector will rely on additional resource support to meet project needs and foster healthy inter-industry connections.

The value of the arts – What does technology get out of it?

To momentarily turn attention to the point regarding the value of the arts to developing technology and the technology sector, a further topic arose during the discussion with Bünte and Liew. After researching several projects and speaking with their creators, it occurred to me that these collaborations often began with the artist contacting the technologists, rather than an engineer reaching out to a theatre maker, to realise their conception to bring AR to the stage. This raised interesting thoughts about artistic integrity and intention, Bünte mused that the passion behind the project may change if its inspiration is not from the artist. The example of a commission was provided, whereby the imperative behind the idea then becomes less about the artistic seed and more about meeting a brief. I suggest, as someone who has worked on commissions in the past, while professional artists are able to find inspiration no matter the source and directive, it is arguable that a pitch that comes from the artist's own muse has a more immediate and fulfilled sense of passion from the outset. With artistic intention a key component to these projects, it may just be the reality that the artist is looking for a new way to express their vision more so than an engineer is desiring to apply their expertise on a stage, virtual or otherwise.

Another line of thought evolved around inspiration and the genesis for these kinds of collaborations, related to previous points around shared language and articulation. An argument was made by Bünte that some technologists, engineers and the like generally have highly sought-after and elevated levels of skill but may not have the experience or desire to find or articulate a creative vision. I took this to imply that it may not be logical, then, for the engineer to naturally look to communicate a creative idea and seek an artist to interpret it into a creative realisation. In any case, the engineer retains the skills and knowledge to express their vision, whatever it may be, through technological means, so the requirement to enlist others is less clear. Conversely, artists *should* be attempting to uncover new forms of expression and test the boundaries of their creativity. Thus, the onus *must* be on the theatre maker to enlist the help of the engineer to realise their creative vision, rather than the other way around. It would, by extension, also fall to the artist to ensure that the vision is communicated throughout the project, adequately to all parties.

The example of a theatre director may provide further clarification. Much like it is the director's responsibility to understand and connect with each of their actors, designers and production staff to bring them on a unified creative journey, it should also be their responsibility to ensure a level of understanding with the language of the technologists to communicate effectively. It is also the director's chore, often as the initiating force, or at least a principal recruiter of a creative team, to approach and enlist the expertise required. Associated with this assumption, that it is the leader of the theatrical component who demonstrates the onus to drive its collaborators and ensure their understanding, Bünte offered an additional point: this skill is also where the artist and/or theatre form has the potential to assist and offer the technology and its experts a benefit. The sensibilities, skills, and confidence to articulate a creative vision and inspire others to join its realisation could assist the engineer. The ability to communicate creatively and influence and inform audiences and collaborators, for example, could aid others to conceptualise and share insights about their work and extend the parameters of how it may be applied across sectors, which is arguably a valuable opportunity the theatre arts and artists can offer.

Distinctions and differentiation – Theatre, gaming, and competing contexts

When asked how they differentiate between creating experiences for a theatrical event, for instance, compared to some of their other work, such as developing games and gaming content, Bünte and Liew identified several distinctions. Liew explained that, from their perspective, games have long been recognised to have an aspect of psychological manipulation that actively trains players on how to interact within a digital system, the aim being to learn these 'rules' to 'win' or 'finish' the game. This training is dynamic, requiring the gamer to understand, explore, and navigate the game world through constant feedback between player actions and system responses. However, for Liew, this interactive, goal-orientated structure contrasts with technology-enabled immersive theatre experiences, for instance, which prioritise immersion over competition, guiding users into artistic visions rather than game-like objectives.

For Bünte, the application of this technology in artistic contexts also takes a different approach to theatrical immersion than gaming. They suggest that an artistic experience immerses participants in someone else's vision, encouraging exploration rather than competition or completion. This difference aligns the theatrical purpose with a more contemplative, poetic experience rather than an interactive quest. For projects in the arts, the goal is often to invite participants to inhabit a space, moment, or idea, creating an emotional or intellectual impact rather than leading them towards a specific outcome. On this understanding, perhaps it is the intention which helps to differentiate. The intention of the immersion in artistic applications diverges from gaming's structural objectives. Theatrical immersions offer participants a unique role, one less about controlling the narrative and more about existing within it. The artist shapes a world that the audience can explore without the pressure of achieving an objective, preserving elements of traditional theatre and resisting gamification while embracing the possibilities of immersive technology. I suggest this does not need to be taken to mean that a theatrical experience cannot have an objective requirement of its audiences; it is simply that the objective would be a part of the experience and not the ultimate goal, which is more aligned to the exploration of a theme or artistic concept.

Technology and exclusivity – Barriers to ongoing collaborations

When asked about challenges facing the intersection of art and technology, Liew offered the issue of 'gatekeeping.' By this, it was taken to mean certain developers perhaps inadvertently restricting the opportunities for collaborative art-tech projects by limiting who can access and experiment with the best available technology. Major corporations, often early adopters of high-end VR or holographic equipment, can set a prohibitively high standard for quality and maintain, in their interests, a too high cost for others to use similar technologies and meet those standards. This exclusivity hampers the broader adoption of these techniques in artistic contexts, such as the theatre.

When only the largest organisations can afford to develop cutting-edge projects, the standard for these experiences remains out of reach for smaller theatre companies or independent artists who wish to innovate in AR/VR and other emerging tools. However, as technology becomes more accessible and affordable, these barriers may begin to break down. Democratised access to high-quality tech would enable a wider range of creators to experiment with immersive environments, leading to a more diverse and vibrant field. This kind of shift in access would not only lower the barriers for smaller-scale creators but also foster new approaches to storytelling, making these kinds of creative experiences more varied, accessible, and reflective of diverse artistic perspectives.

Understanding and distinguishing AR and VR theatre, and ideas on the future

Discussing the differences between AR and VR theatre experiences, the distinction is offered that VR immerses users in fully digital environments, while AR overlays digital elements onto the physical world, contributing a different avenue for enhancing live performance. The point was made that AR could be particularly promising for integrating digital visuals with live theatre, expanding the graphic and narrative possibilities of live performance without requiring audiences to wear headsets. Bünte also provided the perspective that technology needs practical, real-world applications to be meaningful. This led to the consideration that AR presents an opportunity to enhance the traditional theatrical experience: meaningfully adding to the audience encounter by introducing a new kind of stage effect. In contrast to VR, which is seen as an avenue to create a different kind of theatrical experience, situated within a virtual world, effectively isolating users inside their own unique theatrical event. So, AR can enhance shared, live performance experiences, adding digital layers to the physical space that can be seen by all viewers simultaneously in the same way as lighting, sound, set and AV effects are known to do. AR theatre is, then, chiefly seen as the use of AR as an additional tool for traditional theatre, while VR theatre is located as its own kind of theatrical subset. Both exist as expressions of digital theatre.

Further differences between these forms are identified in the practical challenges arising from these projects combining theatre and technology, especially when considering the scalability and audience reach, noted as most evident in a VR experience. Platforms like VRChat, which hosted the *KINetic* production, allow for the staging of virtual performances that multitudinous audiences can access from around the world. However, these digital platforms present unique challenges when used for live performances that rely on co-located audiences. Productions hosted in online locations, designed to facilitate disparate but large audiences, present issues with latency and dropout due to IP restrictions when multiple people 'dial in' from the same location. Latency, the delay between real-time action and its digital transmission, disrupts the immediacy required for live performance, detracting from the sense of presence and immersion. This means that an online VR experience hosted on a centralised virtual platform is ideally placed to produce works for geographically isolated audience members, an entirely different theatrical experience to that of a collocated group of people in a theatre auditorium, for example. This challenge of audience scale when producing VR theatre is similarly noted in the discussion of CREW's works in a previous chapter.

For digital VR performances to succeed at scale, VR technology should continue to improve its real-time capabilities. When latency and IP constraints are resolved, platforms like VRChat could support more intricate, live encounters for collocated audiences that combine physical and digital elements without technical interruptions. The potential for VRChat to host international performances for disparate audiences, though, does demonstrate the adaptability of gaming platforms for artistic purposes, but arguably, the technical limitations currently restrict these platforms from fully replicating the nuances of live theatre. Admittedly, though, replication of the usual theatre experience is not the goal of many VR theatre makers, so it may not always be a valid concern. As VR technology advances, factors such as reduced latency and improved rendering fidelity are likely to enhance its potential for a variety of audiences and audience locations, contributing to its usefulness and further bridging the gap, particularly between VR experiences at scale and live arts.

This conversation with Bünte and Liew ultimately reveals that the ongoing success of integrating these types of, and other, technologies with creative practices such as live performance will depend on the ability to create meaningful collaborative relationships between artists and engineers. Increased access to evolving digital equipment will also broaden its application in this context, ultimately creating cohesive experiences that draw on the strengths of both theatre and technology mediums while overcoming their respective limitations. The potential for shared, meaningful experiences across platforms is vast, but realising this potential requires ongoing collaboration, technological improvement, and a shared vision and passion for how digital and physical realities can enhance theatrical storytelling for an impactful audience experience.

Technology as best practice: AGAM Tamil language theatre - examples of leveraging technology to support the creative arts ecology and advance commercial, social, cultural, and artistic excellence

Subramanian Ganesh is the Founder of AGAM Theatre Lab (AGAM), and Nallu Dhinakharan is the company's Non-Executive Director (Non-ED). I met with Ganesh and Dhinakharan to discuss the company's experimentations with AR plays, in particular, the work *Duryodhanan*, which is described as a world-first "augmented and virtual reality ... Tamil-English theatre production" (Stanley, 2021). The play is available in both an AR and VR versions, as well as in Tamil and English languages. It was created in collaboration with Vostok VR, a virtual reality and 360° video production company, with funding support from the National Arts Council's Digital Presentation Grant for the Arts and the Tamil Language Learning and Promotion Committee. The play is a seven-minute version of the ancient Indian epic, *Mahabharata*, adapted and written by Dr Elavazhagan Murugan and performed as a monologue by veteran Singaporean actor, Re Sommasundaram. AGAM has made *Duryodhanan* available for free from both Google Play and the App Store, where audiences with a smart device can download and experience the AR version in their own homes, and those with a VR headset can immerse themselves in the virtual reality version at their leisure.

Speaking with Ganesh and Dhinakharan at their headquarters in Tanjong Pagar Distripark, it became clear that AGAM is an ambitious company. Ganesh is keen to highlight that it is not specifically a Tamil theatre company, but a company that produces Tamil theatre. The point is taken that it is a diverse group of passionate creatives and arts administrators with a desire for a broad audience and public appeal. One of the aims of integrating new technologies into *Duryodhanan* was to grow audiences and "reach out to the younger generation that are losing touch with this classical art of performance" (Vostok VR, n.d.), by using the technology to entice and interest young people to engage with theatrical experiences in new ways. Beyond audience growth, AGAM also has the core principle of demonstrating alternative business models for creative companies to ensure the longevity of Tamil theatre and culture in Singapore, but also to showcase the potential economic sustainability of theatre companies in general. Founded in 2019, AGAM's leaders bring a business mindset to its management, which has resulted in a vision that extends beyond creative and economic considerations, leveraging technology to embed concepts of social, cultural, and environmental sustainability into its operations.

Cultural, commercial and ecological sustainability – How technology aids theatre

Duryodhanan, Ganesh explains, was the first Tamil play to win a prestigious *Straits Times*' 'Life! Theatre Award,' Singapore's most esteemed professional theatre accolade. The work had three nominations and was the first Tamil language play to win since the awards were inaugurated over 20 years ago, in 2001. The AGAM Founder and Non-ED, inform that the first Tamil play ever produced in Singapore was presented in the 1930s, adding weight to the significance of their play receiving such formal recognition decades later. The company's ambitions to sustain and support the cultural flourishing of Tamil heritage go further; in 2023 they produced what they believe to be one of the first seasons of the British play, *The Play that Goes Wrong*, entirely in the Tamil language, with English subtitles, at the Esplanade Theatre Studio in Singapore.

This Tamil version of *The Play that Goes Wrong* is also an example of AGAM's embrace of new technologies, with Ganesh informing that AI programs were employed in generating elements of marketing content for the production, enabling high-end animations and visuals. Rather than being used as a tool to remove opportunities for artists, it seems that the AI assistance in this case enabled their team to produce and disseminate effective and tailored content in a time- and budget-efficient way. The consideration being not that the AI replaced the work of others, but that the AI enabled a theatre company to produce content they otherwise would not have had the time nor funds to procure in any case.

Beyond critical and cultural achievements, AGAM are also attempting to lead in terms of environmentally sustainable theatre practices, with the assistance of new technologies. In 2022, the company promoted their philosophies based on the concept of 'green theatre' – environmentally conscious and sustainable practices that also push intellectual and creative boundaries in theatre making, borrowing from the established concepts of ecoscenography (Beer, 2021; Beer et al., 2024; Downton, 2024). The work, *Vincent*, championed ecological conscientiousness in its narrative and themes as well as in its creative practices, even tracking its own carbon footprint. The play used projection mapping technology to lower the emissions impact, even after considering the electricity required, and generate digital set and stage components to reduce material usage and waste.

Vincent was partly created to raise awareness of the environmental impact of live theatre and inspire audiences, and other artists, to consider green theatre practices and philosophies in their own lives. AGAM sees value in the sustainability not only of their own practices, but also in the theatre as an industry more generally. Their desires for sustainability, then, are perceived to extend beyond the environmental, Ganesh and Dhinakharan further acknowledging the pathways required for emerging, talented young creatives and the need to encourage them to enter the theatre industry, fostering and growing its future. Along these lines, leveraging their successes partly enabled by the adoption of technology into their creative and business practices, the theatre company has partnered with the Singapore Indian Education Trust (SIET) to provide annual bursaries for up to three promising students to study any theatre or arts management course at local polytechnics, arts institutions or universities.

For AGAM, then, embracing new technologies is a way to advance creative, cultural, economic, and environmental ambitions to pursue their goals of a sustainable theatre company. They are quick to acknowledge that government support in Singapore is strong; for artists and companies like theirs particularly, they note, during Covid when they began their most successful experiments with theatre and technology. As enthusiastic as ever, they made a conscious decision to take the support being offered and generate something that had not been seen before – an AR/VR Tamil language play – exploring the potential of the technology not only to provide an audience experience, but also as an opportunity to grow audiences and impact the theatre industry in Singapore as a whole.

Cost, time, and experience: Lessons when applying AR, VR, and AI in plays

Since the success of their first experiments with technology in *Duryodhanan*, many of AGAM's productions now leverage multiple mediums, live and digital, in multiple areas: from marketing and engagement to design and delivery of the performance environment. Similarly to the other projects detailed in this monograph, Ganesh and Dhinakharan acknowledge the part of government and private sector partnerships in realising their visions, particularly in the nascent stages of theatre/tech experimentation. The significance of industry collaboration and external support is evidenced with reference to *Duryodhanan*, noting that the project was a resource-intensive venture, compared to mounting a traditional theatre production. They caution, what can be created with SGD$20k, for example, in traditional theatre is considerably grander than that achievable with the same amount invested in an AR play. This echoes the sentiments of others working in this space, and the experience of producing the play *Alex* as detailed in chapters above, reinforcing the need for continued investment and access to affordable technologies.

Further referencing *Duryodhanan*, Ganesh offers some practical advice on developing similar AR/VR works in relation to time. They explain that originally the play was commissioned as a 1.5hr adaptation of the source Indian Saga. However, after initial samples of this work in the virtual environment, it was decided that a full-length version was not appropriate for the digital formats. The seven-minute duration was arrived at after a period of experimentation, editing and testing different lengths. Ganesh and Dhinakharan watched each iteration themselves, gauging their own levels of focus or interest to decide whether it was too long or too short.

They advise that seven minutes was a 'sweet spot,' representing a balance between delivering the most captivating and crucial elements of the dialogue and story, with an audience's tolerance for engaging with the digital delivery of the narrative. The producers of this work note that the time limit seemed especially critical for those experiencing the play from their homes via AR effects on their own devices. The way the effects were achieved, by virtue of a handheld smart device in most cases, perhaps dictated the length of time a participant might be able, or willing, to hold up a smartphone or tablet to perceive the augmentations before feeling muscle fatigue.

However, on the day of the production launch it was noted that some participants spent much longer in the VR world. Ganesh and Dhinakharan recall some audience members remaining for up to half an hour in the virtual environment, exploring the space through their headsets, which were set up at the launch venue – a large public meeting place. This speaks to the experiences of CREW, discussed above, noting that agency and mobility in both the virtual and physical worlds are crucial to maintaining an immersive experience. The initial VR audience of *Duryodhanan* experiencing the play at a public hall with wearable devices housed in a large open area, were given the agency and room to move and explore the world of the play in addition to the actor's performance, which they could also view while in the play world.

Contrast this to the AR audience at home, who were limited by the size of the room they were in, the size of the screen they were accessing, and required a weighted prop to be held up to experience the immersion. To me, this further demonstrates the usefulness of pursuing AR theatre using CARL techniques, which removes the burden of a handheld device and brings an audience into a communal performance space to collectively experience the digital augmentations of an AR play. Though, it does limit the project reach by disabling geographically distant participants from experiencing the encounter.

This reflection on *Duryodhanan* and its observable impact on audiences, relating to interest and willingness to stay within the experience, is in some ways converse to other examples above, which have arrived at the understanding that VR theatre is more restricted in its ability to hold audience attention and supplement the traditional audience experience. Perhaps this demonstrates, then, that it is not so much the form but the equipment and how it is utilised that is most influential on the outcomes of the experience. When burdensome devices are required, in either AR or VR theatre, there are associated limits on experience length and audience engagement. Yet, when equipment is collocated in an appropriate venue, the theatrical outcomes are more likely to be sustained, and positive audience impact is achieved.

The future of technology in theatre

When further questioned about the ongoing application of technology in live, theatrical performances, Ganesh and Dhinakharan present as being of a similar mind. For them, the question is not so much how the technology can be applied, as it is or might be, in a live theatre context, but how the technology may aid in developing greater industrial applications for the theatre. Their provocation is to explore opportunities for growing the theatre industry and enabling it to infiltrate other sectors, rather than only adopting developments from other areas into its own practices. For example, Dhinakharan explains, the unique selling point (USP) of theatre is to use narrative to educate/entertain/enlighten and influence. If other sectors want to use this USP for their own advantage, AR technology, for example, can facilitate that transaction and enable theatre to provide new services. The example of the museum sector is offered by Dhinakaran, where he says actors/playwrights can develop AR scenes that are deployed throughout a museum, activated by haptic/motion technology in, on or around a physical part of the collection. It would then be consumed by audiences at each exhibit to enhance their experience – combining theatre skills in narrative and story with AR technology to bring an exhibit to life.

This kind of entrepreneurial thinking presents as the hallmark of AGAM and its leadership team. The critical element is considering not so much how this technology can help theatre in terms of putting on a play, but how it can be used to leverage theatre's USP to grow its utility and application in other sectors, reinforcing the potential for a theatre company to attain ongoing viability and sustainability. Ganesh reinforces that the future of AR/VR and AI technology is most exciting in its industrial applications outside of theatre, which is where the most potential for theatre to grow also lies. Dhinakaran further asserts that people will always want live experiences, audiences will want to be a part of a live event, and makers will want to keep making live events, so if artists and arts companies wish to continue to use this technology, it must be justified. This is the same concern echoed by Bünte and Liew, in the previous section of this chapter.

Dhinakaran notes that during the Covid pandemic, audiences and funding agencies understood why theatre makers were using online and virtual technologies – they had to, so they could continue to reach audiences who were isolated at home. As the pandemic and its lockdowns have ended, artists now need to justify why there is a need to continue to use and apply these technologies. What purpose does it now serve? As Bünte notes above, it cannot simply be for the technology or the artist's own sake. One obvious rationale to continue its use, then, is to pursue technological applications outside of the theatre, but leverage the theatre's USP to broaden its functionality. For Ganesh, the vision is similarly not to use technology to replace theatre practices, but to elevate theatre. From the *Duryodhanan* experience, he highlights that the seven-minute durational limit for an AR/VR work was a crucial realisation, which had to be leveraged to maximise the benefit to theatre without limiting the utility of the technology to the theatrical experience. Reflecting on the comparisons between the two forms, AR and VR, Ganesh cautions that a successful VR immersion has the potential to be more difficult and expensive than achieving an effective AR experience. My assumption of this statement was that AR could be used atop expressions of traditional theatre, while VR requires a completely new virtual world creation.

Extending the discussion, AGAM's leaders infer that AR may be more likely to continue developing as an additional tool for the theatre to draw upon. On this estimation, it is considered that AR has more potential remaining to elevate the theatrical event as we know it, whereas VR has found its place to enable a different kind of immersive, theatrical experience. This is the same suggestion that has been identified in discussions with both the producers from The Doodle People and reflections on the works of CREW and *Alex*. It is noted that neither can replace the appeal of traditional, live theatre, and it is Ganesh's observation that, post-covid, audiences are interested in returning to the communal event of a traditional live performance. Therefore, it is argued that AR technology, particularly CARL, as an effect seen to enhance but not replace or create a different kind of theatrical event, is further rendered an appropriate form to pursue.

Musings on AI and theatre

Turning the focus to AI specifically, it is clear companies like AGAM are already finding a utility that enhances their ability to deliver successful creative outcomes through the development of marketing content, for example. Shifting to the future, Ganesh and Dhinakharan offer the example of *Oti Uttam*, a 2024 Bengali film featuring an AI avatar of 1960s film star Uttam Kumar, who died in 1980 of a heart attack at age 53. Acknowledging the ethical considerations of employing AI technologies to bring back to life a deceased actor to star in a film; and considerations around intellectual property, replacing a role that may otherwise go to a living actor with that of a dead person; and even links to the concept – and legal considerations – of the right to be forgotten; Ganesh and Dhinakharan confirm it is less about what the technology enables us to do, but what artists, producers and audiences decide *should* be done with the technology. For these innovators, it is the creative industry and its audiences that must decide the ethics and ethical limits of how the technology will be applied.

On a more immediate level, AGAM proves that AI already has a useful application in theatre. The company has used AI not only for marketing, but also to assist in refining the sound characteristics for their musical productions, employing AI pitch correctors to aid performers and enhance their vocal qualities, enabling them to achieve their utmost musical abilities.

In this respect, they do not perceive AI as a threat to theatre, but as another tool to assist them in reaching their creative aims. However, they do note a significant pitfall in current AI technologies, particularly the ever-topical large language models, for their works.

As a company that produces Tamil language plays, it seems the racial bias noted in the historiographic chapter of this monograph is not the only recurring obstacle for the use of AI in diverse theatre contexts, but language bias also impacts its effectiveness. Ganesh and Dhinakharan report that attempts to use AI and large language models in languages other than English, or even to assist with translation of texts from other languages into English, are very problematic and yield consistently low-quality and incorrect results. Using current AI programmes in multi-lingual settings, in this theatre context at least, does not yet work on a practical level.

Technology, art, and philosophy: Ho Tzu Nyen – Using art to understand and examine the most complex implications of our technological future (past and present...)

Ho Tzu Nyen is an esteemed artist known to work at the intersections of visual art, technology, film and theatre. One of Singapore's most respected contemporary artists, Ho is recognised throughout the world as an innovator and provocateur, previously the subject of several publications, articles and interviews. With discussions of particular works, such as *The King Lear Project* (Chui, 2009), investigations of process (Ho & Slater, 2023), reviews and reflections of projects (Ha Thuc, 2021; Pek, 2022), and his own academic writings (Ho, 2007), Ho is no stranger to being the focus of research discourse. Humbled by the opportunity to meet with such a visionary, I found my way to Ho's studio in the Geylang area, where we discussed his works and practice, theatre, art, the human condition, and the place of technology in our ever-changing world.

Poetic justification – Investigating technology with/through art

I asked Ho about his interest in AR/VR and AI technology, given the previous findings that artists concerned with engaging these technologies in their practice would also have a curiosity in this side of the experiment. However, Ho's response as an artist was less definitive, expressing a deeper desire for understanding the nature of the medium chosen to work with, rather than an interest in the functional thing itself. This strikes me not the same as simply an interest in technology, but a complex inquisitiveness driven by a need to understand the technology to deal with it, as Ho expressed, "on its own terms." Unpacking this standpoint further, it appeared to me that this was not only a desire to understand the technology and how it might be used in a practical sense to enable the creative vision, but also an attempt to fathom the cultural, philosophical and social implications of its evolution. Put another way, this may be understood as attempting to unravel the impact of these technological developments on the human condition through artistic practices.

Furthermore, to this point, Ho places emphasis on the need for scepticism to accompany any kind of curiosity that may drive the adoption of technology in art. So, not embracing the technology with the art carelessly or without purpose, but investigating its potential positives and negatives on the human condition, as fundamental drivers to any creative exploration. It could be understood that this position should be a guiding force no matter the medium, meaning that any work relying on AR, AI or VR technology – or any other technological example, for that matter – would necessarily require the same rationale. Perhaps naïvely, I wanted to know how Ho translates this scepticism to his audiences – in what way is Ho able to encourage those who experience his works to also consider the more profound impacts this kind of technology is, was, or may have on their existence in this world. I say naïve because the answer is inherent in the experience itself; and clearly articulated by Ho to an audience through the act of participating in his works of art as an audience member.

However, regardless of my inherent naivety, Ho's graciousness provided me with an appropriately articulate response. From this artist's perspective, whatever the subject, theme or meaning the artist explores in the work, this naturally diffuses along intangible lines of influence and understanding through to the audience. Ho prefers the term diffuse in favour of any kind of 'trickle down' analogy, as there are criticisms to be made of terminology that could place the artist atop, or above, their audience. The desired imagery is of a level dissemination of the thematic enquiry, rather than an instructive, or dictatorial, didactic moralism of messaging. While audiences are integral to the exchange inherent in any artwork – it could even be argued that the art does not exist without the audience – Ho notes that they change with each work, and each iteration/viewing of any particular artwork. For this reason, the question is not necessarily how the artist translates their intention directly to the audience, but perhaps more crucial is the potency of the artist's internal vision and the rigour demonstrated through the connection they express with their creative subject. If this artistic integrity, for want of a better term, is strong, then the impact and influence on any audience will reflect that strength.

As an example of investigating the implications of technology on the human experience through a project that also explores the application of technology in a creative context, Ho turns to the 2021 showings of his work, *Voice of Void*, billed as a VR experience with an anime aesthetic (YCAM, 2021). The encounter drew inspiration from the history and controversy surrounding Japan's WWII experience and the place of the so-called 'Kyoto School' network of philosophers, who helped shape Japanese intellectualism and thought throughout the 1930s and 1940s. The project was presented in collaboration with the Yamaguchi Center for Arts and Media. While some may perceive VR technology as an enabler, providing users the opportunity to 'enter' worlds beyond their physical plane of existence, for Ho, the reality of a virtual world is more akin to the oppression and removal of freedom experienced by populations under Japanese occupation during WWII, than it is a gateway to any possible freedoms in a digital world. The contestation is that VR is often framed around the concept that it enables participants to 'enter' into another world. However, for Ho, this is troubling and should be accompanied by the counter-consideration: the fact that this 'other world' takes away the participant's reality.

Technology and perceptions of agency

Ho explains that there are four worlds within the Kyoto philosophers' theatrical VR experience, *Voice of Void*. Each scenario is linked to the fate of one philosopher, yet all are problematic: some lead to death, some to ethical or catastrophic compromise, and others to situations that result in the loss of liberty and freedom. Audiences can choose which of these worlds they participate in, which provides a sense of agency. However, the reality is that there are only ever the options of these pre-determined four worlds and therefore the outcome of whichever choice is made by audience members is already decided. *Voice of Void*, then, was an expression of tools for discipline rather than a portal into another world. The world of the experience overtakes the audience's reality, with the VR headsets literally 'blinding' the participant to any possibility beyond the pre-defined narrative of these four Kyoto School philosophers. The point is also made by Ho, that there is agency in asking an audience to sit at a distance and watch, as happens in a traditional theatre performance. I take this to mean that they can go in and out of the world at their pleasure, allowing their mind to wander, gaze at the lamps in the ceiling or the programme in their hands, or turn and whisper to the person next to them. Conversely, asking audiences to enter the artist's virtual world and confine them to only the images projected in front of their eyes is potentially the height of removing freedom and agency. The VR promise of agency, it is asserted by Ho, is rendered a fallacy.

In *Voice of Void*, the perception of agency was proposed even further, with movement linked to particular narratives. A sitting audience member was placed within a calm teahouse, able to experience a certain philosopher's teachings and influence. If the audience members were to lie down, their virtual world shifted to prison, sharing the fate of the left-wing philosophers who dared to challenge conservative thought and question the morality of increasingly totalitarian and ultranationalist policies. When audiences stood, they were concurrently taken on an ascension into the heavens, enabled to fly among the clouds with young Japanese pilots tasked with executing the deadly orders of those generals strategising in the teahouses that appeared when the audience sat. Ho also describes a hidden, secret element of the narrative, tucked away as a kind of 'Easter egg.' A room that, if found, provided audiences with the opportunity to hear the voices of the Japanese masters. The artist describes this room as the most punishing, as it can only be experienced in complete stillness. Any movement by the audience, taking them out of the hideaway. This is a deliberate design, the technology fully demonstrating the analogy of lack of agency in Japan at that time – any movement at all, and you lose the opportunity to participate in the narrative.

Co-presence: Audience and other. Classifying multi-form experiences

I was keen to understand how Ho classified his works of art, as someone who is known to traverse creative genres, from cinema to theatre and visual arts. I wanted to comprehend what made a work such as *Voice of Void*, for example, more theatrical than filmic. Perhaps this is a result of so many successful transdisciplinary projects, but the desire to demarcate clearly between labels was less interesting to this accomplished artist. For Ho, the distinction of form was less appealing than a consideration of the concept of *theatrical*. It is less about developing a theatrical experience, as it is concerned with what elements could be seen to make an experience theatrical. In Ho's estimation, theatricality is accompanied by the notion of being looked at/ watched by another, which requires an element of co-presence between artwork and audience. In this way, his artworks could be considered installations but are just as easily replicated in theatre festivals or performance venues. I note the connections between this concept of co-presence and the discussion of liveness as an inherent quality of theatre, connecting to the concept of CARL and its requirement for co-located audience and actors.

The element of co-presence that Ho refers to, does need to be 'real' presence. This was taken to be a distinction between theatre and film, for example, where the audience is not in the same space as where the story unfolds, but rather watching a recording of the edited and distributed movie. For the *Voice of Void* VR experience, then, while the animations, or even dialogue of digital characters and narrations, may have been pre-recorded and edited, the audience is co-located with the narrative as it is told with their involvement each time. Their agency, or at least perception of agency, contributes to the element of 'real' presence, being able to literally move between worlds and influence how they experience the story as it unfolds. Yet, the notion of presence is further interrogated by Ho, who insists that artists also need to push the boundaries of what presence can mean, particularly now that presence can be represented virtually and/or by digital augmentations. Ho posits it can also mean internal presence: the presence of your own consciousness.

Adjacent to the notion of presence, then, is the concept of the 'other.' For theatricality to exist, there must be a sense of the 'other' that can be felt by the audience. This sits well with the notion of co-presence and its importance to the aspect of liveness, which has already been discussed as an integral element for a theatrical experience to be achieved. For the act of theatre to exist, the perceptible existence of a present other must be realised. Exactly what that means for virtual theatre, or theatre in virtual environments, is still open to contest. Further complicating the equation is the advent of AI, which raises additional considerations about the meaning of 'other' and not only whether it extends to the awareness of an internal presence and recognition of one's consciousness, but also whether an artificial intelligence can provide the facility of the 'other' and be considered to convey its own 'presence.'

To my mind, this opens potential possibilities about the place of audiences altogether – if AI can provide an equivalent to the sense of presence, then co-presence can also be replicated. The entire experience of theatre can be generated through digital means, replacing audiences or performers, vice versa or both, to produce experiences that infer the inherent interactions of theatre, and the exchanges of information that occur between human bodies through the experience, but are not produced by humans. The question then becomes, what is the purpose? The result is an example where computers could effectively be creating theatre for computers, rendering humans obsolete. That is, surely, a terrifying prospect.

Predictions for future technology art collaborations

The immediate future for Ho involves the use of both AR and AI technologies. Upcoming works promise to leverage these mediums to further push the limits of what we know and understand about ourselves, our histories and our futures. Ho offers that there is potential for AR to open possibilities for theatre and theatrical events, collaborating with CGI experts to challenge and provoke the concept of actor and acting, tackling one of the most controversial possibilities of the technology to the form: is a human even required for the art of acting? When questioned about the motivations behind a future project such as this, the point is made that it is difficult to distinguish between using the technology to explore its implications on the arts and the world, compared to simply investigating its utility in a practical sense – Ho stresses that to do one of these things, inevitably does the other.

The limitations of employing developing technologies, such as AI, were also discussed. While Ho notes that they would make use of AI technology if it were more advanced, the time will come where its usefulness will grow to their practice. Though, Ho also addresses the perceived limitations of AI as somewhat of a fiction, declaring the more a person works with it, the more ways emerge to bypass those limitations.

Fundamentally, it seems that Ho's vision of the future is somewhere between the present and those things that we do not yet know. Ho proposes that we need to change our thinking about AI, for example, which is currently preoccupied with commanding the technology to do something for us that we already have a way of doing, or to carry out a process that we can already carry out to get a result we could already arrive at. I take this to mean, that we are applying AI in accordance with our old ways of thinking and have not yet found the inspiration to use the technology for true innovation. Ho agitates that artists, engineers – everyone – should be attempting to uncover what AI can do that arrives at a new result we may not yet have even conceived, and developing new ways to conceive of those results.

An alternative application of AI is offered by Ho, suggesting that despite any future functions of the technology, we already have the option to ask artificial intelligence applications to present multiple other possibilities for something we have already created. Ho instructs that AI has an ability to generate all the possibilities, or versions, of something that an artist is only capable of creating one way. By feeding that singularity into an AI process, artists should be able to uncover ways to expose an audience to the multiple possibilities of that work. But, to arrive at a point where AI can assist humanity in realising unknown potentials, humans must first find a way to enter a productive relationship with this technology. The complication for humans, Ho advises, is always found in attempting to navigate multiplicity and accept a diversity of realities. Yet, if we are to coexist with the technology, we must find a way to live and work with it that is positive and healthy.

To conclude with AR versus VR and R – A comparative reflection on the plus 1x3 experiences at Singapore's ArtScience Museum

Discussing, researching and reflecting on the use of AR, VR, and AI in live performance consistently led me to question 'why?' Why should this technology be used in performance, and what is the difference in experience created compared to traditional theatre practices? What is the rationale for using holograms to create a CARL experience, for example, when actors in costume or puppets with puppeteers could arguably achieve a similar result? Why insist on an audience entering the artist's tightly controlled virtual world for a VR immersive experience, when they could alternatively walk through a space in the real world populated with real-life theatrical elements?

Outside of the automatic response – because we can – attempting to satisfy in my own mind, the differences and distinctions that may provide points of clarity on this topic, I attempted to undertake a comparative exercise and participate in three separate experiences, each representing a key form for this research. Those encounters were the AR and projection mapping exhibit, *Future World: Where art meets science*, the VR immersion, *Sen VR*, and the traditional exhibit, *The World of Studio Ghibli*. All three of these projects were concurrently presented at the ArtScience Museum at Singapore's Marina Bay complex.

A short summative description of each work

Future World: Where art meets science (Future World) represents an AR experience. It was created by the international art collective, teamLab, a company formed in Tokyo, Japan, in 2001. teamLab is a "multidisciplinary collaboration of engineers, computer graphics animators, mathematicians, graphic designers, architects, artists, and computer programmers … [known] … for its electrifying installations that transcend boundaries between gallery, public space, and popular entertainment" (Lee, 2022, p. 2). *Future World* is a collection of curated experiences, dispersed between two themed sections: *City in a Garden* and *Exploring New Frontiers*. As the audience moves between each experience, literally delineated by walls as each is housed within a separate room/space, they are treated to a mixture of: visual effects animations, participant-created augmentations and physical sensation.

The visual effects animations include flowers and leaves that appear to fall from the walls and move in a flurry as they fall near the audience's feet. An effect achieved through projection mapping. The augmentations are of the audience's own creation, with participants able to draw objects that are scanned and then become a part of the animated projections. The physical interactions are enhanced by projection; for example, participants can remove their shoes and travel down a slide while animations of sea creatures surround them or balance across suspended wooden slats while avian animations encircle from above. This experience could be classified as CAR, as the animations are projected within the audience's real-world environment, but the encounter is more an installation than a theatrical experience, with most of the augmentations pre-recorded and without human performers.

The *Sen VR* experience was created and directed by Keisuke Itoh. During the encounter, the audience meets Sen, a sprite character representing the spirit of tea, in a private teahouse room, surrounded by a tranquil Japanese garden. Seated individually and wearing VR goggles, each audience member enters the VR world and is led through the universe and cosmos with Sen singularly – this is not a communal experience. Participants hold a real Japanese teacup, from which Sen emerges, for the entire performance, providing a physical artefact for them to encounter. Itoh explains "In this story, the user meets Sen, an incarnation of tea, born into the world from a Chawan held in both hands. For the first time in its life, it encounters and interacts with nature and others. Sen experiences the joys of life and a great deal of suffering. His 'life' is no different from ours. He is us" (2024). In contrast to the moving experiences of CREW, *Sen VR* is a static encounter, the effect of movement provided only by a turn of the head, whereby a participant may look around the tearoom, or the cosmic universe Sen takes them throughout the journey. I should also note that the narrative was non-verbal, and while the Sen character did emit some cute, anime-like sounds, there was no distinct dialogue apparent in the work.

The World of Studio Ghibli is an example of the 'R' from this section's title – the 'real' instance of a creative experience. It is more akin to a traditional art exhibition, though it does offer some level of interactivity. The display first appeared in Japan in 2013, since travelling to South Korea, Hong Kong and Bangkok throughout the years (Seet, 2024). Presented in Singapore for the first time in 2024, this is one of the largest iterations of the work and includes recreations of famous scenes and characters from some of the Studio's most internationally well-known films, including *Kiki's Delivery Service*, *Howl's Moving Castle* and *Spirited Away*. A curated collection of memorabilia, life-size models and interactive scenescapes, audiences can walk through recognisable locations from their favourite films. Regularly throughout the experience, there are opportunities for attendees to take a photo amongst the set and characters and recreate famous moments from the stories, placing themselves in the frame. Opportunities range from giving the impression that they are Pazu catching the falling Sheeta, from *Castle in the Sky*, to sitting next to No-Face on the train from *Spirited Away*. Replica, life-size models of characters and scenes are installed so that audiences can take a place within them and have their photo snapped, ultimately appearing in their own staged image as if they were in the scene from the film and a part of the action.

Sen

The *Sen* VR experience was an instructive one: its serene Japanese aesthetic, high-quality animation, and meditative music evoked an atmosphere of 'Zen' – a feeling of calmness and peace – which heightened the experience and maintained my captivation throughout. Yet, the physical reality of the heavy headset and the visual bleed at the bottom of the wearable goggles did influence engagement. At the outset, my vision and, therefore, my focus was distracted by the view of my lap below my goggles, as they did not fit as snuggly as they could have. In VR, physical constraints directly influence the perceived quality and audience acceptance of the duration of the work. *Sen* ran for 15 minutes, which seemed optimal for this non-verbal story VR experience, causing consideration of the findings of AGAM theatre and audience engagement within VR environments that are driven by a dramatic narrative.

Twice as long as AGAM's AR *Duryodhanan*, the quality of the *Sen* performance and the complete encapsulation within the world of the tea sprite, enhanced through its soundscape and refined animations, seem to indicate that while time within a digital narrative, particularly one that does not enable broad physical movement, is likely limited, it can be unique to each experience. There is also an interesting further investigation surrounding the cultural considerations when reflecting on these encounters, particularly in comparing the example of *Duryodhanan* with a work like *Sen*, deriving its heritage from a Japanese context, which Paul Roquet argues brings a unique set of contextual understandings to VR experiences (2022).

The *Sen* experience may also prompt deeper consideration of the point made previously that AR has a more obvious potential to enhance aspects of traditional theatre. For instance, in a CARL experience, the aim is to provide augmented elements in real-world settings: the integration of the virtual in the physical world is crucial. Unlike VR, it has been claimed, which isolates participants within a headset, CARL experiences rely on creating an interaction that remains grounded in the tangible. Thus, the materiality of the physical environment contributes to the realism and emotional impact of the performance, offering a depth of experience that it is argued, perhaps VR alone cannot replicate.

However, in this *Sen* example, holding a physical cup while navigating a VR environment added a tactile layer to the event, serving both as a symbolic object as well as an integrated part of the theatrical narrative. This is something that may not be so easily achieved in a non-immersive CARL play where the audience is seated collectively within the auditorium but separated from the theatrical elements onstage, real and augmented. This underscores a further consideration for a VR theatre experience: *Sen* proves that objects can be incorporated with the same physical impact and consequence as props in an immersive theatrical setting using traditional dramatic elements, where touch, weight, and interaction deepen the reality of the performance.

It may be interesting to further consider the labelling of *Sen* as a theatrical experience. Though *Sen* created a captivating narrative journey partly due to its pleasant and rich virtual environment, there remain questions around the notion of co-located presence between actor and performer that has been said to define live theatre. Indeed, the only actor in *Sen* was a computer animation. However, this leads to the further consideration of Ho's comments regarding the understanding of presence, and the need to re-determine its meaning in the face of technology, perhaps with particular attention to the notion of self, or internal presence, and a consideration of whether a fully digital character meets the threshold for presence. Furthermore, there were multiple people in attendance for each showing of *Sen*, each seated on their own and separated from one another by the distance between each chair, but also isolated by virtue of having their field of vision encapsulated by the wearable devices.

So, while the audience members were certainly present for the *Sen* performance, were they more akin to the seated audience of a film? Is *Sen*, therefore, a theatrical performance, or more accurately a film or even visual art installation? Perhaps the question is, though, not so much whether it is theatre or visual arts or film, but as Ho suggests, why should it be restricted to any of these creative expressions? It is a VR experience, and attempting to locate it within existing forms is potentially a distraction from enabling the evolution of the technology as an emerging medium to express the human condition in its own right.

Future World: Where art meets science

Future World, labelled an AR projection mapping exhibit, in some ways highlights the inherent strengths of projection-based experiences as visual rather than dramatic. Along these lines, it worked incredibly well as a visual art exhibition but may have limited utility as a drama experience, which it admittedly was not designed as. However, the projection mapping may be something that could be leveraged to enhance a CARL theatre experience. Arguably, as a form of visual art, projection mapping succeeds in creating striking images that blend with architectural elements and invite contemplation as well as the possibility for direct interaction. It is perhaps this element of direct interaction that proves most interesting in developing and applying to the theatrical form and specifically immersive theatre.

As its own medium, *Future World* demonstrates that projection alone may lack the exchanges in dramatic narrative storytelling that defines live drama, potentially serving instead as a static background or passive element within the performance. To enhance a theatrical experience, though, there is one element in the way projection mapping was applied in *Future World* that presents some potential. How the work enabled participants to draw and then scan their own animations to be included as part of the visual display, is an interesting component for a dramatic work. Particularly for an immersive AR theatre work, the ability to directly influence the visual elements heightens audience interaction and enables individualised components, and therefore individuals, to influence and actively participate in the narrative.

The World of Studio Ghibli

Unlike *Sen*, where the audience exists in a sealed, sensory-enclosed experience, and *Future World*, where audiences could observe but not physically encounter the animations, the Studio Ghibli exhibit places physical, touchable replicas of beloved story elements within reach – keeping in mind, many parts of the exhibit were labelled "do not touch!" However, even for those elements of the exhibit where touching was not allowed, the potential tangibility of real objects, spatial arrangements, and atmospheric details offer a sense of connection with the physical space that, arguably, digital replications struggle to emulate. Physical installations evoke the memory of touch and spatiality, bridging the gap between audience and story in ways that digital mediums may not yet be able to replicate.

However, AR technology could be leveraged to create a performance experience where the evocation of atmosphere, touch and space inspired by a physical exhibit/object might be replicated but without the risk of damage that seemingly requires the "do not touch" warnings, then a truly wonderful experience for audiences could be created. This would represent the best of both worlds and may be a future outcome for a CARL experience, using holographic images to replicate the tangible. In this respect, the potential for AR in live performance lies in its ability to overlay digital information on real spaces, merging the imaginative possibilities of VR, for example, with the tangible aspects of physical environments represented in this Studio Ghibli exhibition.

An AR-based experience could allow audiences to interact with both real and virtual elements without losing the grounding effect of the physical world. This approach would enable a deeper sense of presence as audiences navigate and manipulate both real and augmented objects within a cohesive narrative space, bridging the gap between visual and dramatic arts. Add to this the potential of haptic technology to reproduce sensorial reactions in the body, and the possibilities increase even further. Additional consideration should also be given to the *Sen* experience, and its physical cup as integral to the encounter – perhaps the full physical replication of *The World of Studio Ghibli* is not required, with its associated carbon miles and resources and materials needed to transport it across the globe, but a selection of smaller examples of objects as inferences, supplemented by the digital augmentations to fulfil the larger and more sustainable experience.

A conclusion to this section

The evolution of VR, AR, and projection mapping within arts encounters continues to challenge our understanding of what constitutes immersion, theatre, live and mediated performances. Experiences like *Sen* demonstrate VR's capacity to create serene, visually stunning worlds, yet also reveal the medium's limitations in offering physical comfort and real-time performer interaction. While VR may excel in visual and auditory immersion, its reliance on heavy, restrictive headsets and pre-recorded content may be seen to limit its effectiveness as a broadly applicable tool for live theatre, interactive or otherwise.

Physical installations, such as *The World of Studio Ghibli*, underscore the importance of tangible, real-world elements in creating a sense of presence that may enhance an experience, particularly if immersion is desired. These corporeal exhibits offer audiences a connection to the material aspects of their world, anchoring them in an environment that feels immediate and real. The success of these installations suggests that future immersive and other theatrical experiences may benefit from hybrid approaches – mixed realities – that blend physical environments with digital augmentations, enhanced by haptics that can simulate the tangible as part of the virtual encounter. Pursuing hybrid experiences may present the most opportunities for future developments. Experimentations with AR technologies evidenced in encounters such as *Future World*, particularly for immersive theatrical experiences, which can combine the most effective elements of virtual, augmented and physical effects, are likely to generate impactful audience encounters.

References

Beer, T. (2021). Ecoscenography. *Theatre and Performance Design, 7*(3-4), 149–151. https://doi.org/10.1080/23322551.2021.2005908

Beer, T., Rixon, T., Garrett, I., & Goh, A. (2024). Embedding ecoscenography into performance design pedagogy: Three practice-based approaches. *Theatre, Dance and Performance Training*, 1–23. https://doi.org/10.1080/19443927.2024.2345609

CENFENG. (2023, January 16). Chinese New Year 2023: Meet the legend of the Nian dragon. *CE Noticias Financieras.* https://www.proquest.com/wire-feeds/chinese-new-ye2?ar-2023-meet-legend-ni2?an-dr2?agon/docview/2766417395/se-2?2?accountid=13380

Chui, J. W. Y. (2009). Interview with Ho Tzu Nyen. *Theatre Research International, 34*(3), 307–309. https://doi.org/10.1017/S0307883309990319

Downton, K. (2024). Putting the theatre green book into practice: Sustainability, pedagogy and the conservatoire. *Theatre, Dance and Performance Training, 15*(3), 429–444. https://doi.org/10.1080/19443927.2024.2380840

Gary, S. C. P. (2013). *Dynamics of Governing IT Innovation in Singapore: A Casebook.* World Scientific Publishing Company. https://ebookcentral.proquest.com/lib/qut/detail.action?docID=1389093

Ha Thuc, C. (2021). What is South East Asia? Emancipatory modes of knowledge production in Ho Tzu Nyen's Critical Dictionary of Southeast Asia. *South East Asia Research, 29*(1), 1–15. https://doi.org/10.1080/0967828X.2021.1877091

Ho, T. N. (2007). The afterimage – traces of otherness in recent Singaporean cinema. *Inter-Asia Cultural Studies, 8*(2), 310–326. https://doi.org/10.1080/14649370701238839

Ho, T. N., & Slater, B. (2023). Honest in the Digging: An Interview with Ho Tzu Nyen. *Southeast of Now, 7*(2), 135–149. https://doi.org/10.56159/sen.2023.a916550

Ibrahim, Y. (2017, October 26). *What happens when Arts and Technology come together in Singapore?* https://opengovasia.com/2017/10/26/what-happens-when-arts-and-technology-come-together-in-singapore/

Itoh, K. (2024). *Sen.* ArtScience Museum Marina Bay Sands. Retrieved November 5 from https://www.marinabaysands.com/museum/exhibitions/sen.html?gad_source=1&gbraid=0AAAAADFjxDoD0OnVcMbG9afKVydA_vz3N&gclid=EAIaIQobChMIzc2Lj-zDiQMVQA2DAx3OnhKXEAAYASAAEgLFGvD_BwE&gclsrc=aw.ds

Lee, L. (2022). *Worlds Unbound: The Art of TeamLab.* Intellect Books Limited. http://ebookcentral.proquest.com/lib/qut/detail.action?docID=6942200

Liew, M. E. (2022, December 8). Integrating tech with the arts for a more vibrant global arts scene. *GovInsider.* https://govinsider.asia/intl-en/article/integrating-tech-with-the-arts-for-a-more-vibrant-global-arts-scene

National Arts Council. (2022, February 11). *Singapore: The National Arts Council's Inaugural Arts X Tech Lab Helped Artists Reimagine Their Practice with Technology* https://www.proquest.com/wire-feeds/singapore-national-arts-council-s-inaugural-x/docview/2629079167/se-2?accountid=13380

Pek, Y. S. (2022). Review of Ho Tzu Nyen, "The Critical Dictionary of Southeast Asia," 2017–ongoing. *NMC media-n.* doi:10.21900/j.median.v18i1.865

Roquet, P. (2022). *Immersive Enclosure: Virtual Reality in Japan.* Columbia Univ Press. https://doi.org/10.7312/roqu20534

Seet, M. (2024, July 24). ArtScience Museum Presents 'The World of Studio Ghibli' Show This October, Here's How to Get Tickets. *TimeOut Singapore.* https://www.timeout.com/singapore/news/artscience-museum-will-present-the-world-of-studio-ghibli-show-this-october-012324

Sipahi, E. B., & Saayi, Z. (2024). The world's first "Smart Nation" vision: The case of Singapore. *Smart Cities and Regional Development (SCRD) Journal, 8*(1), 41–58. https://doi.org/10.25019/dvm98x09

Stanley, S. (2021, February, 17). Tamil Theatre with a Virtual Reality Twist. *The Straits Times.* https://www.straitstimes.com/life/arts/tamil-theatre-with-a-virtual-reality-twist

Tan, J. (2007). Nian – the story of the Chinese New Year. *Caribbean Quarterly, 53*(1/2), 222–230. https://www.jstor.org/stable/40654987

Vostok, V. R. (n.d.). *Take a Journey on First Tamil Volumetric Drama in Asia with Holograms.* Vostok VR. Retrieved 31 October from https://www.vostokvr.com/hologram-ar-volumetric-performance-duryodhanan

Wu, E. (2006, January 26). The Dallas Morning News Esther Wu Column: With traditional flair, dancers roar in the Lunar New Year. *Knight Ridder Tribune Business News,* 1. https://www.proquest.com/wire-feeds/dallas-morning-news-esther-wu-column-with/docview/463042814/se-2?accountid=13380

YCAM. (2021, January 21). *A new project by Ho Tzu Nyen, an acclaimed artist from Singapore* https://www.ycam.jp/asset/pdf/press-release/2021/voice-of-void_en.pdf

6

NOT NECESSARILY A CASE STUDY, A CHAPTER WITH A NORTH AMERICAN EXAMPLE AND GENERAL DISCUSSION OF AI AND THEATRE

While examples of the current use of AI in a live performance context have been identified throughout the case studies above, and opportunities for its future potential to further enhance the creative process proposed, one of the considerations when penning a book about technology, is how quickly the field changes. For this reason, it is helpful to take some time to investigate the implications of such technology beyond the practical and the tangible. The following chapter, therefore, takes more of a philosophical approach to the technology and its place in the world. As it stands, the most prominent example of AI in the current public discourse is large language models, such as ChatGPT, which artists have adopted in their technology-experiments since its earliest days. Although, creatives have been exploring the potential of this kind of technology for much longer, with America's Annie Dorsen incorporating chatbot technology into a seminal work as early as 2010.

Less than five years ago, the power of AI large language models now freely available to the public, for example, was largely inconceivable to most people. Shifting just a few years later, at a recent fundraising lunch targeted at upper-middle management and small business owners from around my home city of Brisbane, when those sharing my table discovered I was working on a monograph that included discussion of AI, I was met with gushing accounts of how these models had improved their efficiency and diminished the resources required to complete many of their daily tasks. From using online software to write official HR letters to underperforming employees to crafting legal-sounding correspondence intended for adversary businesses, these managers of industry told tales of reducing the need for expensive

DOI: 10.4324/9781003521907-6

administrative staff and cutting legal costs by virtue of drafting their own strongly worded letters without having to engage professional counsel. When I asked them, "was the advice accurate? Who checked the content before the documents were released?" I was met largely with blank stares.

I would then account my own experiment with large language models, particularly GPTs engineered specifically for academic writing. As a test, I asked one of these publicly available programmes to write a section for an academic journal, using the premise that technology was shaping live performance in a positive way. The programme performed wonderfully: an entire chapter generated – though, not a long chapter – detailing the main points and arguments of the topic, replete with references to leading theories and citations for supporting evidence, just as I had requested. However, upon closer inspection, I realised I had never encountered most of the names cited in the chapter and could not recall any of the key sources publishing or producing the works that were referenced. A cursory check revealed the AI had, in every example, made these things up. And, while the words and sentences sounded very persuasive and academic on the surface, on closer examination, it read more like a politician's oration – very little substance, superficial meaning, and hidden contradictions. It took me two hours to vet, correct, and improve the GPT's offering. I felt it was less efficient than writing from scratch myself, but this feeling could also be attributed to not having yet 'trained' the programme to more accurately reproduce my desires – or perhaps, the programme had not yet trained me…Although, several months later, the result from a similar test with a newer version from a different developer already produced better results, though still flawed.

There were some at the table who brushed aside the implications of my experience, refusing to question the validity and accuracy of their own creations using AI large language models. But, for the majority, there was a realisation that the perceived convenience and potential of the technology had, in fact, been too good to be true. I could only wonder about the implications for them if the content of their time- and cost-saving letters were to be challenged formally, and I received the distinct impression they were wondering the same thing. A further example of a lawyer from Melbourne, in the Australian state of Victoria, who had been referred to that jurisdiction's legal complaints body after using a popular legal AI platform to generate a case list to be used in court, without verifying its accuracy: in reality, none of the cases provided as precedent by the AI service existed (Taylor, 2024b). In the same jurisdiction, caution around the use of AI has gone even further, with Government child protection staff banned from using open-source AI GPTs in their work, not only due to privacy concerns around entering personal case data to prompt the programme, but also considering the fact that responses generated by the AI algorithm were found to downplay the seriousness or potential harm to a child (Taylor, 2024a). This technology still has some way to go.

For now, the enhanced speed and efficiency of AI in this context is yet to find a way to also replicate the expertise and accuracy of human experience and knowledge, without the ability to discern and critically analyse its own perceived intelligence. There seems to be a general consensus, though, that the programming to overcome any shortcomings may soon follow, and my scepticism will become a moot point and render me the person at the table laughing on the other side of their face. However, there are other critics who agree that placing too much stock in the future capabilities of AI could lead to a downfall, declaring this technology "makes so many mistakes that it [is] questionable whether it would ever reliably solve complex problems" (Mickle, 2024).

A discussion of AI large language models, though, is simply the current de rigueur, and there are multiple other applications of AI in numerous contexts. In the case of theatre, while there are examples of works using large language models and similar programmes as part of their creative frameworks, they are only one possible application of AI. Perhaps, though, as Ho suggests above when discussing new technologies and works of art, theatre offers the most opportunities not in its adoption of AI into its practices, but in providing the poetic exploration, philosophical consideration and audience provocation to consider the ethical, moral, cultural and social implications of embracing AI, including large language models, in all facets of human life, such as the legal and commercial scenarios discussed around the abovementioned luncheon table.

The three Cs of AI in artistic practice: Creative, collaborator, concept

Rather than discounting a discussion on technology as obsolete before it begins, though, perhaps it is a useful exercise to examine the ways in which AI is being deployed by theatre makers and other artists in general terms, both currently and potentially. While the technology, its effectiveness, accuracy and accessibility may change rapidly, one consideration is that the ways in which it may be applied can be classified in broad enough terms that those classifications do not shift so swiftly, and any advancements may, regardless, be allocated within these definitions however things change and evolve. In practical terms, it seems that AI's use in theatre and the arts more generally can be classified into one of three categories: AI as creative, AI as collaborator and AI as concept – the three Cs of AI in artistic practice. Specific examples in a theatrical context are given here, but analogous roles could be identified across the creative and performing arts spectrum and, indeed, across sectors outside of the creative industries.

As creative, AI is placed to develop, generate or invent creative works and creative content, for example, in much the same way a writer, director or actor would contribute to a process. In this facility, a script may be written by an AI large language model; a written work may be analysed and assessed by an AI programme and changes, edits or rewrites provided by it; or model dialogue may be fed into a data system that then generates substantive lines of a play that are delivered by the computer itself through a simulated – or replicated – human voice, either as a kind of narrator or via an animated character. In this respect, the labour of human creativity can be considered outsourced to the AI technology; even though the initial prompts or ideas may come from a carbon-based, biologically living, human person, it is the computer – for want of a better term – that produces the creative product, which may or may not then be performed/produced/presented by human or computer means.

AI as a collaborator is perhaps the most obvious application of this technology in current theatre practices. This includes the use of programmes that track, sample and correct the pitch of an actor's singing voice in a musical context; the application of image editing software to generate marketing content or stage decorations, or deliver vision effects such as projection and visualisation enhancements for a live mediated performance; or assess a play script and offer notes or summaries or statistics of likely success amongst certain demographics, but not amend or contribute to the creative document itself. In this context, AI technology is used to enhance the human contribution or enable the artist's creative vision to be realised without driving the content or form of that vision from a principal position.

There is an argument to be made that the example of image editing software and similar applications of AI technology is more than collaboration and could potentially replace a human creative from a visual arts and graphic design perspective. As artists and creative industries practitioners, we should remain very sensitive to this and ensure our practices do not disadvantage others in the field. However, despite their potential for inter-/intra-/cross-disciplinary application, this example is offered specifically for theatre and live performance, with the practice of theatre making as the primary concern. In a previous chapter's example, it was demonstrated that applying AI technology in this way at AGAM theatre did not, in practice, have the effect of removing an opportunity for a graphic designer or visual artist, but allowed a theatre company the opportunity to develop content it would otherwise not have generated in any case. In reality, the AI contribution enabled the theatre maker to improve their graphic design capabilities, through techno-collaboration. So, AI as collaborator for one discipline, may be regarded AI as creative to another.

The categorisation of **AI as a concept** is directly linked to the subject or themes of an artwork. For example, plays that explore AI through plot, character and/or story fit into this understanding, as well as those that discuss, explore or demonstrate the application of the technology in past, present or future contexts. Investigating the moral, ethical, and social impact and function of the technology also meets this classification. Works that exemplify AI as a concept may also employ AI as creative and/or AI as a collaborator. Indeed, for each category, the example may or may not include or incorporate elements of another of the three Cs of AI in artistic practice.

The inclusion of AI does not need to be a main or driving element of the work where AI as a concept is concerned, but any production that touches upon AI in its dramaturgical world can be considered to include examples of AI as a concept, though it may not be an example itself overall. The extent to which it is an example is relative to the centrality of the AI technology to its plot, character and/or story. So, a play that cursorily mentions AI in its narrative may demonstrate AI as a concept at that particular point, but it may not be considered an overall exemplification of AI as a concept production, where AI is a central character or driving theme.

Further, an AI as concept artwork does not itself need to utilise AI technology to meet the description. For example, in October 2024, the play *AI May* premiered at PIP Theatre in Brisbane's inner suburb of Milton. This work, written and directed by Amy Chien-Yu, is squarely an AI play that demonstrates AI as a concept without using any AI technology in its delivery. The play's AI effects were achieved very successfully using traditional scrim and projection devices to provide the impression of intuitive touchscreens, and the AI robot character was portrayed entirely convincingly by a real human actor, Clarise Ooi.

A further consideration is how an AI as a concept work may be different from a sci-fi play. In practice, one may be an example of each and the other. After viewing *AI May*, it also occurred to me that as recently as 5–10 years ago, this work would have been easily categorised as a sci-fi play, but in fact may now simply be considered a contemporary drama. The technology it purported to showcase was no longer a fiction but a reality. The assumption being, though available, the technology was not incorporated into the play due to reasons of resourcing. The effects provided by traditional theatre equipment and design are more accessible than incorporating literal elements of the technology referred to, presumably due to the currently high cost of purchasing an actual robot and predictive computer interfaces, which would surpass the likely budget for most independently produced stage plays.

AI and Annie Dorsen – A North American example who is a world leader and authority on the theory and practice of this technology in live performance

In 2010, renowned theatre maker and technology artist, Annie Dorsen, created the world's first production of 'algorithmic theatre,' titled *Hello Hi There*. The work centred on the use of chatbot technology from the 1970s, generating dialogue for an expectant audience not through large datasets known to current GPTs, but by selecting words "from a list of pre-written sentences that [Dorsen] had assembled and laboriously organised into massive decision trees" (Dorsen, 2023). These kinds of technologies, word trees and chatbots, have been deployed in several other examples, their influence on art also explored by Aleksandra Przegalinska and Tamilla Triantoro in their book, *Converging Minds.* (2024)

However, Dorsen's seminal work with algorithmic theatre is arguably a genesis for AI theatre, and in January of 2023, Dorsen premiered *Prometheus Firebringer* at Bryn Mawr College in Pennsylvania, described as having "on one side of the stage everything ... made by commercially available AI products: A set of AI-generated theatre masks, animated by AI-generated computer voices, perform[ing] scenes made by GPT-3.5 (the same model that runs ChatGPT [at the time]). On the other side of the stage, [Dorsen] give[s] a talk that reflects on some of the questions these models raise" (Dorsen, 2023). This work is, then, a fine example of all three Cs of AI in artistic practice.

Dorsen (2019, p. 113) provides the following definition for algorithm:

> an algorithm is a procedure, a series of discrete steps that can turn an input A into an output B. An algorithm does not have to be computational. In the classic examples, a recipe for baking a cake is an algorithm, and so are directions to the airport. Computerised algorithms are, of course, much faster and more complex than handmade ones — and they really do, unlike girls, run the world.

The interest, then, for Dorsen was to apply this formulative process to the creation and production of live theatre, "to see what would happen if one applied a strict rules-based process to a notoriously analog and humanist art form ... while accounting for those traditional aspects of theatre, however flexibly interpreted, that make it theatre: narrative development, character, spoken language, and so on" (pp. 113–114). The concept of AI theatre, then, is perceived as a kind, or perhaps subset, of algorithmic theatre, particularly where the AI theatre is AI as creative – the application of an algorithmic process, undertaken by technology, to create a theatrical experience for human audiences.

The audience experience is understandably central to the experiment, mirroring the accounts provided by makers across the case studies of this monograph. Dorsen also places emphasis on this and relates audience engagement to the notion of curiosity. In earlier chapters, the requirement for artists and technology collaborators to share an interest in both the art and the technology is identified as key to successfully generating these kinds of experiences. Dorsen's notion of curiosity can also be seen as an expression of this.

However, the concept of curiosity and interest is extrapolated by Dorsen beyond the relationship between artist and collaborator, found also as crucial to the interaction between artist and their audience. Dorsen is quoted as preferring:

> the idea that the performance can take place on an equal footing between performer and audience, rather than the performers or the director having something they try to communicate, something that they know already but the audience doesn't know … the notion that we can all come together with an equal curiosity about what will transpire on this particular evening.
>
> *(Jouve, 2016)*

Speaking of the algorithmic theatre work, *Yesterday/Tomorrow*, Dorsen confirms that the curiosity and shared interest required by an artwork's creators is also present for those who encounter the work. The unique experiences offered to audiences by Dorsen's experiments with algorithmic theatre and AI are said to reshape the entire relationship between human audiences and technology (Felton-Dansky, 2019). This may be a critical point in attempting to ensure, predict or understand the place of technology in future theatre productions and other works of art. The point is reinforced, that the success or otherwise of continued experiments with technology in this context not only depends on audience acceptance of its use, but also on their interest and curiosity in its adoption. It is one thing for artists and their collaborators to be interested in using the technology; it is quite another for audiences to share that desire.

In *Yesterday/Tomorrow*, "technology neither amplifies nor mediates human performances-it conducts them" (Gillette, 2016, p. 443). The show consists of three actors, at the outset singing the song *Yesterday* by the Beatles, before transitioning into *Tomorrow* from the musical theatre piece, *Annie*. It is reported that each performance is unique, with the transition from one song to the other dictated by a computer program, an algorithm that conducts the singers from one ballad to the other via a different song-path during each performance. Kyle Gillette (2016) recounts:

> At first, the singers and the music they read repeated *Yesterday* several times without any obvious changes. Then a sound, a tempo, a duration shifted, along with the notation the audience could read above the performers. One singer's part introduced the word chin at the end of a complete *Yesterday* verse; then other words appeared. Harmonies and melodies strayed as tones, note lengths, and phrases varied. Disjunction accumulated over time. Each mutation iterated each previous mutation, gaining complexity, approaching chaos. The familiar phrases of *Yesterday* decayed—not dissonant, but shifting according to invisible rules that did not seem like rules at all.

In this example, Dorsen achieves a sense of delegation to the technology. Rather than a musical director, conductor, writer or lyricist dictating the narrative journey of the play, it is the programming that leads and decides the words that will be sung by the actors. This is also an interesting experiment in improvised theatre, with the actors and creators just as oblivious to what comes next and how it might end as the audience is, no doubt a further expression of Dorsen's belief in the potential for audience and maker(s) to share in the curiosity of how technology might influence the creative product.

A further consideration might be found in relation to the programme itself, and whether it is arguable that the engineer responsible for its programming might ultimately be considered the creative in this example, rather than the technology. Yet, a converse consideration is that Dorsen, as the one responsible for applying the computer engineer's programming in this way, is truly the creative genesis of the work, rendering the technology partly AI as a collaborator, rather than strictly AI as creative – it is used to realise Dorsen's creative vision, as well as iterating its own creative offering, implementing elements of its own 'AI creativity.'

Canvassing Dorsen's work further, it could be suggested that curiosity in technology and how its digital infrastructure might be applied to, what Dorsen terms the analogue frameworks of live theatre and performance, is not a singular driving force. There is a deeper comment and criticism to be found of the broader impact that new technologies, particularly those algorithm-driven programmes represented partly by AI, are having on society and culture generally and the arts particularly. Dorsen sees an overwhelming, and arguably undeniable, digitisation of modern society underway, heralding the "corrosion of truth, democracy, and mental well-being" (Gill & Dorsen, 2024, p. 19) in broad terms, but more specifically contributing to a degradation of the role of performing arts in particular, and the subsequent cultural, moral, and political implications this has for society (p. 20). At the crux of it are questions surrounding the commercially driven imperatives behind these technologies, often developed in consideration of outcomes such as productivity, scalability, distribution and efficiency. Gill and Dorsen (p. 20) contest:

> Promising the development of new audiences, broader accessibility to artworks, and new revenue streams for artists, digital platforms may actually produce many of the same damaging outcomes we have seen in other contexts: the reduction of everything into "content," further concentration of corporate control over creative expression, the erosion of authoritative human discernment, and the intensification of human labour.

Here, we see the crucial place of theatre and the arts in questioning the role of new technologies, not only experimenting with them in their practices.

Much like Ho warns above, the artist and maker should not adopt the technology for its own sake but must approach any project with a level of scepticism aimed at much broader social and cultural implications. This affirms the notion of AI as a concept as potentially one of the most critical to advancing society, ensuring that artists, audiences, and the communities they represent remain aware and engaged with the world we are creating, increasingly relying on technology to facilitate our very existence.

Another recurring theme of Dorsen's work, also seems to be the notion of ephemerality. Extending upon the understanding that theatre has the ephemeral at the core of its live experience – no two performances are ever the same, given the subtle shifts, changes, timings and ad-libs actors and audience offer and experience that can never be replicated outside of the moment they occur – this element also presents as a hallmark of many Dorsenian productions. *Yesterday/Today* generated unique song-paths between its eponymous tracks each time it played, just as no two versions of the inaugural algorithmic theatre, *Hello Hi There*, resulted in the same pathway along the pre-defined language-tree being generated. Similarly, the 2013 production, *A Piece of Work: A Machine Made Hamlet*, is explained to "effectively essential[ise] a different version of [Shakespeare's] *Hamlet* each time it is algorithmically produced – although each performance also renders itself *in*essential [original emphasis] to its ensuing iteration: an inoperative template ... for each equally ephemeral performance to come" (Cartelli, 2016, p. 433). Tangential lines are drawn to the use of AI large language models in other contexts, where the same prompt provided multiple times generates a different output in each instance.

One of the enduring curiosities of this kind of AI-driven algorithmic theatre, then, is the ability to generate unique, irreplicable and ephemeral experiences for audiences, using pre-programmed computer models driven by pre-defined digital rules.

A short conclusion to this section

This chapter and the works of Dorsen provide an opportunity to consider more deeply the notion of AI as a concept. Perhaps the most cunning aspect of Dorsen's works is its ability to question and comment upon the use of AI and its greater social, political, ethical and moral impact while simultaneously employing it as both creator and collaborator. The application of AI technologies and the thematic investigation of their impact on theatre, art, society and the world at large is still an incomplete map, rife for experimentation and provocation through and by artists and their artforms. An artist like Dorsen realised the potential disruption this technology would cause to human creativity and existence many years before the advent of open access

GPTs, applying the technology in theatrical contexts prior to the incursion of AI large language models across commercial and creative sectors becoming the hot topic of discussion around the table. While the technology will continue to enable new ways for artists, theatre makers and their collaborators to connect with audiences, it also remains critical that theatre and other artforms continue to question, challenge and interrogate the place of AI in all of its capacities – creative, collaborative, and as thematic content – and the impact, real and potential, this had/has/will have on society as a whole.

References

Cartelli, T. (2016). Essentializing Shakespeare in the Shakespeare aftermath: Dmitry Krymov's Midsummer Night's Dream (As You Like It), Matías Piñeiro's Viola, and Annie Dorsen's Piece of Work: A Machine-Made Hamlet. *Shakespeare Quarterly, 67*(4), 431–456. https://doi.org/10.1353/shq.2016.0055

Dorsen, A. (2019). Plato, procedures, and artificial everything. *TDR: The Drama Review, 63*(4), 113–120. https://muse.jhu.edu/article/740506

Dorsen, A. (2023, August 30). The dangers of AI intoxication. *American Theatre.* https://www.americantheatre.org/2023/08/30/the-dangers-of-ai-intoxication/

Felton-Dansky, M. (2019). The algorithmic spectator: watching annie dorsen's work. *TDR: The Drama Review, 63*(4), 66–87. https://doi.org/10.1162/dram_a_00875

Gill, S., & Dorsen, A. (2024). The work of art in the age of digital commodification: the digital political economy of the performing arts. *TDR: The Drama Review, 68*(1), 19–50. https://doi.org/10.1017/S1054204323000618

Gillette, K. (2016). Germinal/yesterday tomorrow. *Theatre Journal, 68*(3), 443–446. https://www.proquest.com/schol2?arly-journ2?als/germin2?al-yesterd2?ay-tomorrow/docview/1877820940/se-2?2?accountid=13380

Jouve, E. (2016). Of theatre and algorithm: Interview with Annie Dorsen. *Miranda* (13), Online. https://doi.org/10.4000/miranda.9454

Mickle, T. (2024, September 25). Will AI be a bust? A wall street skeptic rings the alarm. *New York Times.* https://www.proquest.com/newsp2?apers/will-2?ai-be-bust-w2?all-street-skeptic-rings-2?al2?arm/docview/3109514028/se-2?2?accountid=13380

Przegalinska, A., & Triantoro, T. (2024). *Converging Minds: The Creative Potential of Collaborative AI.* CRC Press. https://doi.org/10.1201/9781032656618

Taylor, J. (2024a, September 26). AI ban ordered after child protection worker used ChatGPT in victorian court case. *The Guardian,* NA. https://link.gale.com/apps/doc/A810226764/AONE?u=qut&sid=bookmark-AONE&xid=77035089

Taylor, J. (2024b, October 10). Melbourne lawyer referred to complaints body after AI generated made-up case citations in family court. *The Guardian,* NA. https://link.gale.com/apps/doc/A811849076/AONE?u=qut&sid=bookmark-AONE&xid=067ad82a

7

A CONCLUSION TO THIS BOOK

It is evident that the application of emerging technologies, such as AI, AR, and VR, within a live theatre and performance context is an evolving consideration. While there are many lessons that can be identified in the history and experiences of works demonstrated by companies like CREW, using more established technological tools such as those associated with VR experiences, the full potential of AI and AR for the theatre, performance and live arts is yet to be realised. It is argued that some of the tenets for a successful VR experience – such as audience mobility, perception of the inside and outside worlds, and the considered enrolment and exiting of audiences as participants – should be applied in all immersive encounters, regardless of their technological modality. However, the requirement for these elements to create a successful audience experience for non-immersive environments is not so persuasive.

There are, however, commonalities across technologies and creative forms that are rendered useful regardless of whether AI, AR, or VR is being employed within individual projects. Wherever collaboration is required between artists and technologists, the examples investigated here are unanimous in the requirement for shared interest and passion, developing an understanding and belief in the project that can transcend disciplinary peculiarities and misunderstandings. The need for realistic economic and practical support, particularly in these early stages of technology and art experimentation, is also clear. A commitment to developing and updating infrastructure should be taken seriously, and institutional backing for experimentations with technological adoption in the arts is crucial to ensure the sector's advancement and to secure our cultural heritage. This is required to sustain

DOI: 10.4324/9781003521907-7

the sector until technology advances and access to evolving equipment and the programmes that make it work becomes more widespread. The prediction is that these technologies will need to play an increasing role in how the live arts are generated, created, realised, presented and disseminated.

In terms of the theatre specifically, AR technologies present the clearest opportunities for adoption into its traditional practices. While it is conceded that VR technology has a prominent place in the developments of immersive theatre and has already established its usefulness in this regard, requirements such as participant mobility and fit-for-purpose site-specific spaces render it suited to developing its own unique form. It can be understood, then, that VR theatre and immersive VR experiences are more likely specific types of digital theatre/digital performance rather than elements that can be easily subsumed by traditional theatre as an additional technological tool. Conversely, the opportunities afforded by virtue of AR technology, especially notions of CARL, may offer substantial developments to the long-established dramatic form. The ability to incorporate AR effects in much the same way as conventional lighting and AV components are embedded, offers a tangible and realisable possibility to enhance traditional methods of theatrical storytelling with digital augmentations.

The concepts of CAR and its live counterpart, CARL, are useful to navigate the possible applications of AR in a live performance context. CARL allows for technological effects to be embedded within established dramaturgical frameworks, while preserving those appealing elements that can be considered foundational to the dramatic form: communal experience and liveness. However, there are ongoing debates around how technology, particularly VR environments that enable digital locations and virtual presence, have shifted and changed the meaning and understanding of notions such as co-location, shared space and the concept of 'live.' For now, it will be affirmed that virtual worlds cannot yet replicate the same physical and environmental interactions and encounters that physically co-located audiences and performers share.

With predictable developments in visual imaging improving how virtual worlds are displayed and advancements in haptic technology, for example, shifting the possibilities for the digital to replicate the tangible, this assertion of the irreplaceability of the live, communal arts experience may find itself challenged in the future. Perhaps, then, rather than rely on the ineffability of the inherent interactions between audience and performer of the live theatrical event, the craft would do well to ensure it is at the forefront of these unavoidable developments, positioning itself to leverage any breakthroughs to enhance its reach and influence the progress of the technology, rather than simply be influenced by it. This creates multitudinous possibilities, including the potential for bringing the unique, ineffable experience of theatre and live performance to audiences who would otherwise be denied the opportunity, whether through distance, means or social and political disadvantage.

In terms of AI, there are three categories identified for its inclusion within a live art and performance context: AI as Creative, AI as Collaborator and AI as Concept. The inclusion of the technology as a concept is perhaps the least problematic in terms of its impact on traditional creative practices, with the ability to explore AI as a theme and subsequently consider its impact on society on a broader scale in much the same way a play or any artwork may unpack any issue. As a collaborator, AI is already contributing to the artform in several ways, such as enhancing vocal performances, generating marketing collateral and contributing to script development. The moral and ethical considerations here are evidently more significant, with concerns related to the place of the human in these collaborations and their displacement or superseding by the technology, as well as concerns of ownership and attribution where AI is used to generate what was, previously, exclusively human work.

Perhaps more starkly, though, are the ethical and moral considerations surrounding AI as Creative, where the place of the human and humanity's previously sole domain over creativity are challenged even more forcefully. In the works of Annie Dorsen, computer programs are seen to take the place of content creators and even performers, with theatrical experiences generated and presented by the AI itself. Ultimately, though, the level to which this technology interacts with, or overtakes, the place of the human will and must be decided by artists, their audiences and society more generally.

And now, just for fun, a conclusion written by AI. I'll leave it to you to decide whether the Skynet takeover is imminent:

Conclusion: Toward the Future of AI, AR, and VR in Live Performance

The integration of AI, augmented reality (AR), and virtual reality (VR) technologies into live performance represents a transformative evolution in the way audiences engage with art, narrative, and the performative experience. Through this investigation, it has become clear that while these technologies hold immense potential to expand the boundaries of traditional theatre, their success depends on striking a delicate balance between technological innovation and the foundational principles of live performance: presence, liveness, and human connection.

AI and the New Role of the Performer

Artificial intelligence has begun to redefine the creative process in live performance, offering tools for real-time interaction, improvisation, and generative content creation. By integrating AI into dramaturgy, performers can engage in dynamic exchanges with digital systems, blurring the line between human and machine agency. However, AI's role must be carefully calibrated to support, rather than overshadow, the human performer. Live performance thrives on the immediacy of human presence, and AI's value lies in its ability to enhance this presence, providing new layers of interaction without supplanting the essence of human creativity.

AR and the Fusion of Real and Digital Spaces

Augmented reality bridges the physical and digital realms, creating a hybrid environment where performers and audiences can interact with both tangible and virtual elements. AR has proven particularly effective in live performance by enhancing the physical stage without isolating the audience from their environment. This blending of real and augmented worlds fosters a sense of wonder while maintaining the tactile and social dimensions of live theatre. As AR technology advances, its potential to create immersive, site-specific experiences will redefine the relationship between performance and place.

VR and the Enclosure of Immersion

Virtual reality offers unparalleled opportunities for creating fully immersive experiences, transporting audiences to entirely new worlds. However, VR's promise comes with challenges, including physical discomfort, technological limitations, and the isolation of participants within headsets. To achieve its full potential in live performance, VR must move beyond its current limitations, integrating tactile, social, and embodied interactions that align with the principles of theatre. The future of VR in live performance lies in its ability to create shared, multi-sensory experiences that are as engaging as they are immersive.

The Human Element in Immersive Technologies

Despite the sophistication of AI, AR, and VR technologies, the essence of live performance remains rooted in its human and social dimensions. Theatre and live performance are inherently communal acts, drawing their power from the shared presence of performers and audiences. As these technologies continue to evolve, their success will depend on their ability to amplify, rather than replace, this fundamental human connection.

Technological integration must also be democratized to ensure that artists from diverse backgrounds and resources can access these tools, fostering innovation and inclusivity across the field. Breaking down barriers to entry—whether financial, technical, or creative—will allow a broader range of voices to contribute to the evolution of live performance in the digital age.

A Future of Boundless Possibilities

The use of AI, AR, and VR in live performance is still in its infancy, with creators, technologists, and audiences collectively shaping the vocabulary and grammar of this hybrid art form. This period of experimentation is vital, as it allows for the exploration of new storytelling techniques, audience interactions, and sensory experiences. The future of these technologies lies not in replacing traditional forms of theatre but in enhancing and expanding them, providing tools for deeper engagement, emotional resonance, and shared exploration.

As live performance continues to adapt to the possibilities of AI, AR, and VR, it faces a profound opportunity to redefine the boundaries of artistic expression. By harnessing the transformative potential of these technologies while remaining grounded in the essence of human connection, live performance can chart a path forward that is as innovative as it is timeless—a testament to the enduring power of storytelling in all its forms.

(Academic Writing GPT, 2024)

Reference

Academic Writing GPT. (2024). *Write me a conclusion to a high-quality research monograph investigating the use of AI, AR and VR technologies in live performance.* ChatGPT. Retrieved November 27 from https://chatgpt.com/g/g-xUsBarC1Z-academic-writting

INDEX

For Product Safety Concerns and Information please contact our EU
representative GPSR@taylorandfrancis.com
Taylor & Francis Verlag GmbH, Kaufingerstraße 24, 80331 München, Germany